Protecting Children

A PRACTICAL GUIDE

Janet Kay

CASSELL
London and New York

Cassell

Wellington House
125 Strand
London WC2R 0BB

370 Lexington Avenue
New York
NY 10017-6550

www.cassell.co.uk

First published 1999

British Library Cataloguing-in-Publication Data

A catalogue record for this book is available from the British Library.

ISBN   0-304-33415-4 (paperback)

Designed and typeset by Ben Cracknell Studios

Printed and bound in Great Britain by Redwood Books, Trowbridge, Wiltshire.

Contents

Foreword

This book illustrates how textbooks can be exciting, interactive and accessible to learners. Unlike so many authors who tell us what we need to know, Janet Kay has sought to involve us in our own learning and to help us integrate our experience with practice. Janet's considerable experience as a child protection specialist and as a lecturer shines through. *Protecting Children* not only addresses what those involved in childcare need to learn but how they learn. It is relevant to anyone providing a service to children and is an excellent introduction to the complex world of childcare and the painful issues of child abuse and protection.

If you are planning to read this book you may be a childminder, a play leader, a foster carer or a student on a professional training course studying to become a social worker, teacher, police officer or nurse. Whatever your involvment in childcare, *Protecting Children* will act as an excellent introductory reader. You may be registered as an NVQ (National Vocational Qualification) candidate. Whatever your role you will be wanting to build on the knowledge and experience that you already use in your day-to-day work with children and their families.

As consultant editor it has been a delight to work with Janet Kay, an author who has risen to the challenge of producing a book which is both informative, well structured and user-friendly. She has recognized that her audience will bring their own considerable personal experience and knowledge, and therefore demonstrates a respect for the reader throughout the book. As she guides you to a basic understanding of child protection issues and relevant theory she constantly reminds you to reflect on your own experience. I trust that you will be reassured by her recognition of the emotional and practical implications of being involved in the painful and difficult realities of working with children and families where abuse has occurred.

Janet has taken into consideration the fact that many readers themselves have experienced some level of abuse in their own childhood and must inevitably struggle with the strong emotional responses provoked by working with children and families. She emphasizes the importance of making sure that you get support for yourself.

Throughout the book you are provided with opportunities to link to your own circumstances, settings and the particular situations of children in your care the information and ideas presented. The numerous case studies and examples drawn from practice provide illustrations to enable you to think more broadly. The 'chance to think' sections encourage readers towards reflective practice and help them to transfer general skills and knowledge to new circumstances.

Reflective practice requires us all to recognize and include our own experience and then to consider and amend our behaviour and actions to meet the needs and demands of the service and our theoretical understanding. Many of you will not have been involved in formal education for years or may have had negative experiences of academic learning – the idea of theories and textbooks may be quite terrifying. Try to relax and enjoy reading this book, where theory is presented in easily digestible chunks and made relevant to the real world of childminders, foster carers and residential social workers.

When you have read the book and completed the exercises you should find yourself able and confident to satisfy many of the requirements for a vocational qualification at level 3 or be well prepared for further academic study of child protection literature.

Vocational Qualifications

The material presented in this book has been designed with reference to several units contained in National Vocational Qualifications (NVQs) in England, Wales and Northern Ireland or Scottish Vocational Qualifications (SVQs) in Scotland. The agreed National Standards, which provide the structure for these qualifications, are indicators of best practice and quality services. The book is primarily, though not exclusively, designed to meet the learning needs of National Vocational Qualification candidates. It will be particularly relevant for candidates registered for one of two awards (see Appendix III):

- Early Years Care and Education, Level 3
- Caring for Children and Young People, Level 3

Appendix III outlines which aspects of the Underpinning Knowledge and Understanding (UKU) specified in the Vocational Qualification units of competence have been covered by each chapter. The book as a whole focuses particularly on one unit entitled 'C15 Contribute to the protection of children from abuse'. This unit appears in both qualifications. However, there is considerable overlap with other units found in the mandatory core or optional units of these two qualifications. The identification of how chapters can be linked to the underpinning knowledge should prove helpful to candidates and assessors planning assessments and programmes of learning.

The design and presentation of the material and the use of structured exercises to reinforce and integrate learning makes *Protecting Children* an ideal book for independent study. It is also likely to prove useful to anyone offering training in the area of child protection, e.g. foster carer training or NVQ/SVQ learning sets, as it provides a structure and curriculum for group learning and workshops.

Chapter 1 provides a general introduction to what is considered child abuse and establishes a number of themes which are explored throughout the other chapters. It looks at the issues of changing definitions of and different types of child abuse, personal and societal values, and the need to understand 'normal' child development. These themes are integrated throughout the book and the reader is encouraged to recognize the demands, constraints and choices which they must consider.

Chapter 2 provides more detailed information on the types of abuse: physical, emotional, sexual abuse and neglect with case studies used to illustrate each. The reader will acquire an understanding of each of these categories and recognize the value and limitations of definitions and categories when working with real people and situations.

Chapter 3 provides an essential understanding of the signs and symptoms of abuse which will enable the reader to recognize and articulate concerns for the welfare of any child. The importance of recognizing the limit of the worker's role and the importance of working in partnership with other professionals and parents is also explored.

In Chapter 4, the focus is on how a worker should respond to suspicions of abuse. Checklists of good practice in responding to disclosure, how and when to discuss concerns with parents, recording and reporting information, provide the reader with an opportunity to assess themselves and improve their own style and methods of working with children and families. Many readers will benefit from the simple explanation of the roles of other professionals who may be involved in child protection and an introduction to the formal procedures such as child protection case conferences.

Chapter 5 outlines the different court orders to which a child might be subject and the legislation which governs child protection in the United Kingdom. The principles of the Children Act are described in ways which highlight and demonstrate the impact of the legislative framework – the impact of child protection processes – on individual childcare workers in a whole range of settings. It recognizes the importance of the contribution the reader can make to the monitoring of a child at risk and to the ongoing protection of children.

Chapter 6 provides invaluable guidance on working with children who may have been abused, focusing more on direct work with the child than on the framework or professional network. Unlike many books which might discuss good practice in theory, the author demonstrates an understanding of the considerable strains and demands on childcare workers. Children who have been abused often display difficult or demanding behaviour. The checklist on 'Coping with Difficult Behaviour' is preceded by a helpful reminder: 'Of course it would need an angel to display this level of patience, tolerance and calm all the time, but the guidelines are there as an indicator of the sort of responses it can be helpful to consider when faced with difficult behaviour'. A reassuring thought for anyone who has been involved in caring for children!

This practical 'how to do it' theme is continued in Chapter 7, which focuses on preventative measures and empowering children to protect themselves from abuse and to develop self-confidence. Particular attention is paid to the importance of partnership with parents and themes established in the opening chapter are revisited.

What is so pleasing about this book is the way in which the readers can hear the author speaking directly to them using everyday language, e.g.:

> there are a number of factors that can help you to decide whether a problem
> does exist for a particular child. One of these factors is to be aware of the most
> common sites of non-accidental injuries. When children fall, what do they fall
> on? Children usually damage themselves on their hands, knees and shins during
> falls; elbows and foreheads, noses and chins – in fact all the bony bits.

The author also anticipates that you, the reader, will already have some knowledge and awareness of child abuse and the exercises often direct the reader to discuss with friends or colleagues, compare and contrast or recall what you have read in newspapers. This book serves to remind carers what they already know as well as offering new insights and providing information from research and best practice upon which to build and increase competence.

The author's aim in writing this book is to enable anyone working with children, where abuse might be an issue, to develop sufficient competence to practise at the standard required to achieve a National Vocational Qualification (NVQ) or to provide a basic introduction for professionals in training. I feel certain that she has achieved this objective and hope that you agree.

Linda Jones
Independent consultant and trainer

Preface

This book is intended to provide a basic understanding of child abuse and child protection issues for a range of childcare workers in a variety of settings including childminders, foster carers, nursery workers and playgroup workers. Some sections will also contribute to the knowledge base of candidates for the NVQ in Early Years Care and Education (level 3) and NVQ in Caring for Children and Young People (level 3).

The book is structured to provide the reader with opportunities for self-assessment through a range of exercises in each chapter which can be used to reflect on what has been learned or to research a particular aspect further. The exercises are in sections titled 'A Chance to Think'. Some of the exercises have sample answers for the relevant chapter in Appendix II. The sample answers are not meant to be the 'right' answer. Many of the exercises are used to explore opinions, feelings or ideas and, so, often there is no 'right' answer. The sample answers are therefore provided for you to check on the type of answers which may be appropriate and for you to compare your own ideas and thoughts with another's. Some of the exercises relate to case studies which can be used to explore work practices with children in different settings.

In order to keep the text simple the term 'parents' has been used to describe any person or persons who act as parent to a child. This could include foster carers, grandparents or guardians, or any other person who normally lives with and takes care of the child on a day-to-day basis and who has the prime responsibility for the child's welfare and happiness. The term 'childcare worker' is used for anyone who has care of children other than their own in either a paid or voluntary capacity, whether this is in their own home or outside the home such as a nursery, playgroup, school or crèche.

For further simplicity the practice of referring to a child as 'she or he' or 's/he' has also been avoided. Instead, the child has been referred to as either 'he' or 'she' on a fairly random basis. As this book is mainly aimed at childcare workers who work with young children the term 'child' usually refers to children between birth and 8 years old. However, children are not abused in neatly defined age groups so occasionally the effects of abuse are discussed in terms of older children, adolescents and adults, particularly to demonstrate the long-term impact on the individual of abuse in childhood. The examples and case studies also include children of a wider age range to meet the needs of readers who care for children of different ages, e.g. foster carers.

Although every effort has been made to keep the language simple and uncluttered by jargon, inevitably some words have been used that are rarely heard outside a child protection case conference or court of law. This has been necessary on occasion because the term may be used by other professionals involved with the child, or because the term originates from legislation affecting child protection. In order to clarify jargon, legal terms and so on, a glossary has been included which contains such terms used in the text.

This book is aimed at exploring issues surrounding child abuse and child protection as they would affect childcare workers in a variety of job roles. Many childcare workers work on their own and may not have a supervisor to whom they can refer. Where the need to consult a supervisor or colleague is mentioned, the term 'appropriate person' has been used for those of you who work alone. The 'appropriate person' could mean a foster carer's support worker, or an under-8s social worker, a health visitor or another childcare worker you are in contact with. Essentially, it is always important to have someone to share concerns about a child with if at all possible. If you have serious concerns and no one to discuss them with, contact the duty social work team at your nearest social services department or the National Society for Prevention of Cruelty to Children (NSPCC) to get advice and help on what to do.

The book is meant to be read as a whole. Although some sections may not seem directly relevant to your particular work role with children, they are included to provide a framework for understanding the whole of the child protection process. In Chapter 1 the issue of child abuse will be explored in broad terms in order to try and establish a picture of what child abuse is, how prevalent child abuse is in society and what the causes of child abuse might be.

Acknowledgements

I would like to thank my friends Heather Croft and Howard Upton for lending me their attic and computer, Carolyn Spray for advising me on various points of procedure and the law, and my partner Peter Howell for his support and patience.

Awareness of Child Abuse

Dealing with Your Own Feelings about Child Abuse

Child abuse can be a painful issue to read or think about. You may be surprised at the strength of your feelings in response to some of the material in this book. You may also feel the weight of responsibility that working to protect children places on you. There are many uncertainties in recognizing and responding to possible child abuse and these can add to the feelings of discomfort when dealing with this issue. These feelings are perfectly natural and are found in everyone involved in child protection. It is important to have someone to talk to about these feelings, such as a colleague or friend, while you work through the material in this book. It is also important to be aware of what we are feeling about child abuse, so that our feelings do not get in the way of our contribution to protecting children.

There may also be some readers who have been abused as children themselves. Reading the various sections may revive painful memories, or bring back feelings of sadness and hurt. You may see your experience reflected in the case studies or examples given. Many of you will have dealt with your feelings through supportive relationships, both professional and personal. For those who have not been able to do this yet and who may feel they wish to talk to someone now, there are a number of organizations offering confidential, sensitive support and help to abuse survivors. A list of these is given in Appendix I.

A Chance to Think

 Personal feelings about child abuse are entirely natural and expected from anyone who has contact with abused children. These feelings may be anger and outrage at the damage done to a child and sadness and grief at the child's pain. Other feelings may be more complex. We might feel anxious about our role in the proceedings or about how we will deal with the child and his family. We might not want to see the parents because of the anger we feel towards them. We might feel guilty because we did not stop the abuse earlier or we did not recognize signs and symptoms. We might just wish it would all go away. Feelings about child abuse may be difficult to handle because they are powerful and disturbing.

Exercise 1

1. Write down all the reasons you want to find out more about child abuse. What are your concerns about dealing with abused children?
2. Write down the feelings that you have had when you have read about or been involved with children who are abused. Note how you felt about the child, the parents and any professionals involved. Try and be honest about how the abuse made you feel.

Keep your answers to look at again when you have reached the end of the book.

What Is Child Abuse?

Over the last 30 years child abuse has become one of the major social issues in our society. Since Dr Henry Kempe, an American paediatrician, 'discovered' the 'battered baby' syndrome in the early 1960s child abuse has entered our everyday life through newspaper and television reports.

Child abuse has been the subject of plays, films, novels, soap operas and an endless number of documentaries exploring every aspect of the abuse and protection of children. There is an enormous amount of literature which examines child abuse from every angle. Child abuse scandals have dominated media reporting for days and sometimes weeks at a time. Perhaps the term 'child abuse' has become so familiar that we forget the need to look closely at what it actually means. Everyone has their own image of an abused child. Stop reading for a minute and quickly jot down your image of the abused child, without thinking about it too much. What sort of abuse springs to mind immediately? It may be a child who has suffered physical injuries or sexual abuse. Ask a colleague or friend to do the same exercise. Is their image similar to yours? Try a selection of people and look at the range of images which are produced.

Although Kempe's work was instrumental in bringing child abuse to the attention of the general public, child abuse has always been a feature of society. Changes have taken place in how child abuse is received and responded to and what is seen as abusive, but the abuse of children is certainly not a new phenomenon. The NSPCC was given its Royal Charter in 1894 and in 1889 the first child protection law, the Prevention of Cruelty Act, was passed by Parliament. In 1946 a foster child, Denis O'Neil, was killed by his foster father, a case which strongly influenced the setting up of local authority Child Care Departments. However, despite this progress in recognizing and responding to child abuse, there was no real understanding through the early part of the twentieth century that child abuse might be a widespread problem.

Professionals working with children had few guidelines to help them recognize and respond to child abuse and there were no procedures and policies to help them protect children in a consistent and effective manner. Children with inflicted physical injuries were often simply not recognized as having been abused. Underlying this lack of response to child abuse was a lack of recognition that child abuse existed apart from in the case of a tiny minority. One of the main lessons that has been learned about protecting children is that protection will only result if the adults around the child are able to believe that child abuse really happens and that it is widespread.

Kempe and his colleagues drew attention to the injuries suffered by some of the children they had treated, arguing that there was no other explanation for these injuries than that they had been inflicted by adults. The term 'battered baby' was used to describe these children, although many were no longer babies. Child abuse became front-page news and the public began to be aware that this was a much greater problem than previously thought. This growing awareness of the extent and nature of child abuse has resulted in it becoming one of the main social issues of modern times.

However, although society came to accept that many children suffered physical abuse within the family, other sorts of child abuse were not so readily recognized. Emotional abuse of children was gradually incorporated in professional understandings of what child abuse is, although the extent to which it could cause long-term harm to the child was only gradually discovered. However, child sexual abuse remained more of a mystery for many years, with little professional recognition and understanding of the nature and extent of such abuse. Like the 'battered baby' syndrome, child sexual abuse was seen as a rare and isolated phenomenon.

Twenty years after the 'battered baby' syndrome was recognized, growing professional and public awareness of child sexual abuse resulted in this becoming the child protection issue of the 1980s.

Before we can explore all aspects of child abuse and child protection we need to try and answer the question 'what is child abuse?' You may have already come up with some ideas of the answer to this question, but you may also have found a confusing range of responses from other people. However, in order that we can formulate responses to child abuse which will be helpful in protecting children we need to know just what it is that we are protecting them from. Also, by stating what is abusive to children, we are also making a statement about what is *not* abusive. This involves some notion of drawing a line between different types of child care practices on one side of which is acceptable behaviour towards children, and on the other side of which is abuse. This concept will be explored in detail below.

A Chance to Think

 One of the central problems of working in child protection is the difficulty in defining exactly what is abusive and what is not. Although some child abuse is very obvious, for example, severe physical abuse involving permanent disability or death, some behaviour towards children is more difficult to categorize as abusive or not abusive.

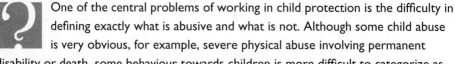 Exercise 2

1. Write a definition of child abuse. Try to avoid listing the different types of abuse or forms that abuse might take. Instead try and produce a definition that will cover all incidents of abuse. Compare your definition with those in Chapter 2.
2. Ask a friend or colleague to write a definition as described above. Compare your definitions. How do they differ? In what way are they the same?

You will probably have discovered that it is very difficult to write an overall definition of child abuse, a problem that many child protection agencies and organizations have been struggling with for years. You may also have discovered that the more people you ask to define abuse the more variations you get on what is and is not abusive. The purpose of the exercise is to try and demonstrate that there is no single definition of child abuse that will always work in all circumstances, all societies and all ages.

 ## Exercise 3

Think back to the punishments meted out to children 30 years ago, when corporal punishment was common in schools and it was not unusual for children to be beaten with belts, slippers and other implements in the home.

1. Would these sorts of punishments be acceptable now?
2. Would you describe them as abusive?
3. Think back to your own childhood or ask your parents or grandparents about the sorts of punishments which were common in their childhood. Would these punishments be used commonly now? Do you consider them abusive?

Definitions of child abuse are considered in more detail in Chapter 2.

Although some types of behaviour towards children would always be thought of as abusive by most people, there are also areas where there may be disagreement about what is and is not considered abusive. There may be shifts and changes over time about what is considered abusive to children, and different cultures and societies may have different views on this matter. As societies grow and develop, the concept of what is abusive to children changes. For example, in Britain in the nineteenth century it was normal for working-class children to work from a young age. Often the jobs were dirty and dangerous, particularly mining and factory work, and it was not unusual for children to be maimed or killed in these jobs. At the very least, these children were denied education, fresh air, leisure and freedom, and were exposed to a lifestyle that could cause long-term damage to their physical and emotional health.

At the end of the twentieth century we would find this totally unacceptable. Or would we? Child labour continues around the world, often exposing children to similar risks to those outlined above. In Britain, it could be easy to point out that child labour is mostly confined to developing countries. However, these developed countries benefit from the low-cost goods produced by child labour, and imports of goods produced at the expense of children's health and well-being continue.

To add to the confusion, different individuals and organizations in the same society may have different views on what is and is not abusive to children. An example of this in Britain today is the debate about corporal punishment of children. The 'no smacking' lobby has been growing for some years, and now there are many parents who do not use smacking as a punishment of their children, and there are also many childcare organizations who support this policy.

For example, many local authority social services departments ask their foster carers to agree to a 'no smacking' policy, and corporal punishment is not allowed in local authority schools and residential children's homes. However, many parents believe that smacking children is not harmful, and use smacking as a method of disciplining their children. Another example is the racist abuse of black and Asian children in British society. If we regard the abuse of children as behaviour or actions resulting in some sort of harm to the child, then the everyday verbal and physical abuse some children are subjected to must surely come under this heading. Yet the racist abuse of children by other children or adults is rarely dealt with as child abuse despite the long-term emotional and psychological harm that can result.

A Chance to Think

 Defining child abuse can be difficult, because there is always some area of uncertainty between what is and what is not abusive. There are many disagreements about acceptable and non-acceptable treatment of children. One example of this is smacking. Although physical punishment of children is still acceptable in our society, physical abuse of children is not. How do we draw the line between the two? There are no easy answers to this question.

Different cultures and different societies have different views on what is acceptable in the way we treat our children. The notion of child abuse is not fixed, but varies over time and between societies. Practices that were normal in one age can often be considered barbaric in the next. In the end we can only fully define abuse in the context of our society at this point in time, although there are some behaviours towards children that would generally be considered abusive most of the time and in most contexts.

Exercise 4

1. Read the six case studies below and try to decide for yourself which you think you would describe as child abuse, and which you would not. Ask a colleague or friend to do the same exercise. Which of the scenarios do you think are most abusive, and which are least abusive? How did you decide? Discuss your decisions with your partner, and compare the criteria you used for making them.

2. Your decisions on whether the child has been abused or not will probably be based on some notion of harm to the child. Look at each case again and for each one write down which of the child's needs are not being met in this situation. Use the list of needs in Appendix II for reference. What might be the effects on the child of not having his or her needs met? Ask your colleague or friend to do this exercise also and compare notes. Compare your answers to the sample answers in Appendix II.

1 Grant is 2 years and 6 months old, and in the last six months he has regularly been having tantrums which involve screaming and throwing himself on the floor, refusing to do as he is told and becoming hysterical if approached. His mother has become totally exhausted by this behaviour and does not know how to deal with it. His father believes that the behaviour is due to lack of discipline, and deals with it by smacking Grant hard on the bottom, and putting him in a room on his own for a long period of time, often until he has cried himself to sleep. Grant's father has also shaken him, sent him to bed without food, and regularly shouts threats at him to try and control his behaviour.

2 Paul is 6, and is the middle child of three. Paul is the only boy in the family, and is considered by his parents to be rather stupid and awkward. They describe him to other people as their problem child, and frequently point out his faults and mistakes, in comparison with the other two children. Paul is usually blamed for any fights among the children. Paul's parents make fun of his appearance, and call him a wimp. Paul does not get the same treats and presents as his sisters, and is often ignored. He confirms his parents' expectations by behaving in a dreary, sulky way, doing badly at school and being clumsy and awkward.

3 Claire is 4 months old. Her mother is only 16 herself, and her father is 18. They live in poor quality rented accommodation, and are unemployed. Claire was born prematurely and was in hospital for a while in the special care baby unit. This

frightened her parents very much. Claire was very small when she was discharged. Her father is out with his friends most of the time, and her mother copes alone. She cannot read and does not understand the instructions on the baby food container. Claire has been back to hospital twice with gastroenteritis and dehydration. She is underweight and looks pale and unhealthy. Her nappy is often smelly because her mother tries to save money by changing her infrequently, and she has dreadful nappy rash. Her mother rarely picks her up because she is afraid of hurting her when she handles her, so Claire spends long hours in the cot, and is usually fed sitting on a sofa with a bottle propped in her mouth by a cushion (prop-fed).

4 Susan is 10. Since her mother left a year ago Susan has often been left to care for her two brothers who are 5 and 6 years old. She makes their breakfast, takes them to school and tries to clean the house. Susan's father is disabled and has limited mobility. However, he likes to go to the pub in the evening and Susan is left in charge. Susan often stays off school herself to help her father and keep him company. She does the shopping and tries to cook. At night she stays up to help her father if he is drunk and needs to be undressed and put to bed. He calls her 'little mother' and says he does not know what he would do without her.

5 Natalie is nearly 4. She lives with her mother in a high-rise flat. She goes down ten floors in the lift to play on the swings in the play area at the base of the building because she is under her mother's feet in the flat. Sometimes she plays in the lift with the older children, and sometimes they go to the shops and steal sweets. Sometimes the older children take Natalie to the back of the flats where they play at 'having sex'. One boy who has been in care always wants to play this game, and he gets Natalie to touch his penis, and tries to push it into her. Natalie does not like this but has not told her mother. All the children play this game now.

6 Rena is nearly 5. She has just started school. She is one of the very few black children in her school. Although she has made some friends in her class, Rena is very frightened by some older boys at the school who shout 'wog' and 'dirty nigger' at her at playtime. They stand around her and laugh at her, and when they have a chance they push her or trip her up. When Rena tried to tell her teacher he told her not to worry because the boys were just teasing her and 'didn't mean any harm'. Rena has had stomach ache every morning during the last two weeks and she cries when she has to go to school.

Child Abuse as a Social Construct

The idea that child abuse can be observed and measured objectively, using a scientific approach, has come under criticism. Some sociologists argue that human beings have complex relationships with each other and the world around them, and that it is impossible to study the social world using scientific principles. Human beings are not neutral – they attach meanings to actions based on the values of the society they live in.

Finding the facts about child abuse is not easy, because child abuse is always viewed in the context of society, not in abstract terms. The expected behaviour of adults towards children varies over time, and between cultures and within cultures. 'Child abuse is a product of social definition. Some sets of facts come to be labelled as child abuse because they go beyond the limits of what is now considered to be acceptable conduct towards a child' (Stainton Rogers et al., 1989, p. 44).

Child abuse can therefore be seen as a 'social construct', in that the values of a social group or culture determine what is considered to be abusive or not. As such, answering the question 'what is child abuse?' will always depend on the social context in which it is being asked.

An example which might help to illustrate this point arose during a training session on child protection. During an exercise, which involved deciding which of a set of case studies described an abusive situation, it came as a surprise that the whole group felt that a particularly bad beating was not abusive. The group felt strongly that the teenage girl deserved the beating because she had been found in bed with her boyfriend, despite the fact that other cases involving much less severe physical punishment were seen as abusive. The group's view of 'what is child abuse?' was shaped by its value system, within which the girl's behaviour was unacceptable, and deserving of punishment.

Different 'social constructs' of what child abuse is result in a range of different explanations as to why children are abused. These are explored later in the chapter.

Institutional Abuse

There are other areas where harm to children is not always perceived as child abuse. Despite efforts on the part of childcare agencies and professionals many children entering the care system suffer harm through this experience. For some children the experience of care can result in a lifetime of instability and unhappiness if suitable long-term arrangements for the care of the child are not successfully made. Even quite young children can experience a rapid turnover of carers or rejection by families with whom they live. Children coming into care after being abused may have difficulty settling with a new family, or may still be attached to their parents, or may have behavioural problems which make them difficult to care for.

Despite the fact that social services departments make every effort to place young children with families, some still remain in institutional care although this is recognized as emotionally harmful. Fostering and adoption placements sometimes break down despite the efforts of all involved. Some children eventually become so emotionally damaged or demonstrate such difficult behaviour that they are not able to join a family with any hope of success. Children leaving care are some of the most vulnerable in society. They are more likely to become offenders or to become homeless than other children. They are also more likely to have long-term difficulties with relationships and in establishing a settled and fruitful lifestyle.

Children entering the care system may also become vulnerable to abuse by their carers. In some residential care establishments childcare practices have been severely criticized in recent years. In others, scandals of sexual and physical abuse of the children have come to light in recent years, with some of the abuse going on for decades. In residential care there has been a growing problem of abuse by other children, who may have been sexually abused themselves.

Non-abusive Parental Behaviour

One way of trying to establish what is abusive to children is to examine what non-abusive parents do with their children, i.e. what normal parenting is. A survey on parenting practices in the 1990s found that 81 per cent of parents hit their children, but 50 per cent felt that they should not do so. The same survey in the 1960s found that 95 per cent of parents hit their children of which 80 per cent thought that it was right to do so (Dartington Social Research Unit [DSRU], 1995, p. 12). Research into patterns of sexual behaviour in families found that many of the behaviours which might be considered to indicate sexual abuse occurred naturally in many households.

These included the child touching parents' genitalia, seeing parents naked, bathing with parents and masturbating. The context in which these activities occurred and the age of the child seemed important. For example, children over 5 start to bath less with parents and parents were less likely to appear naked in front of children as they got older. In some families children would acquire unusual knowledge of sexual activity from watching explicit videos or television programmes, or witnessing sexual intercourse. Although we would probably not recommend such exposure, it would not normally be considered abusive unless the activities had been arranged for the purposes of the adults' sexual gratification (Smith and Grocke, 1995).

There are dangers in trying to define 'normal' parenting. Parenting practices vary widely between and within societies and there is no single blueprint for getting it right. One of the problems for childcare workers may be to try and recognize the value of parenting practices which are different from their own. We tend to believe that the way in which we do things is 'normal' and this then makes other approaches 'abnormal'. We take for granted practices which are part of the pattern of our lives, even if they may be strange to others. For example, it is not unusual for young babies to have their ears pierced in our society. Although this involves puncturing the child's earlobe, causing pain and increasing the risk of an infection, we would not see this practice as child abuse.

A Chance to Think

 Although there might appear to be general agreement on what is considered acceptable and not acceptable childcare practice in a society, this agreement might exclude members of that society whose lifestyles differ from the norm. For example, a commonly held belief is that children are better off in two-parent families. This belief could lead us to believe, perhaps not consciously, that one-parent families do not provide quite such good care for their children as the 'ideal' two-parent family.

 ## Exercise 5

1. Ask your friends and colleagues to describe the ideal family. What sort of family types are seen as normal? Do they tend to be the white two-parent, two-child type of family often seen on television? Why might there be a problem in defining this type of family as 'ideal'?
2. Write down all the negative comments you can remember hearing about parenting practices in different types of families. What sort of families are criticized in this way?

What assumptions are made about these different types of families? Look at the commentary in Appendix II.

Family Stereotypes

One of the problems of making assumptions about different types of families is that the real problems may become obscured. One often quoted example of this is the case of Tyra Henry, a black child who died in 1987, killed by her stepfather. Tyra was placed in the care of her grandmother on the assumption that she would cope with the problems and difficulties of caring for the child. This assumption was partly based on the commonly held belief that maternal figures in Afro-Caribbean families always care for the wider family as normal practice and that they have extensive physical and emotional resources available for this task. When the grandmother became increasingly overwhelmed by the financial and emotional stresses affecting the family, this was not perceived by the social workers involved and eventually Tyra ended up in the hands of her stepfather with fatal consequences (DHSS, 1987).

Assumptions about different types of families are often based on racial or cultural stereotypes. These involve widely held beliefs about certain groups of people that are applied to individuals from those groups without reference to whether they are correct or not. Often these beliefs are negative. For example, it is generally believed that poor working-class families are more likely to beat their children than well-off middle-class families. The danger in such a belief is that the child from the middle-class family may not be protected from abuse because those around her cannot 'see' it happening. Think about other stereotypes you might be aware of and the dangers to children which might result from these.

One commonly held assumption is that disabled children are unlikely to be abused. In fact, disabled children can be more vulnerable to abuse because they may be unable to draw attention to what is happening to them, or they may be unable to protect themselves in the ways outlined in Chapter 7. Disabled children are also more likely to be cared for by a range of adults, e.g. in respite, day or residential care, who may possibly have opportunity to abuse them. Increasingly, it is becoming recognized that disabled children are much more commonly subject to sexual abuse than was previously believed.

Drawing the Line?

It seems that we cannot come up with a clear demarcation line between what is and is not abusive to children for all time and in all places. Child abuse is a social construct and so definitions of such abuse will change and develop over time. They will also vary between cultures and societies. The definition of child abuse is also dependent on the context it is used in. However, despite the difficulties of defining child abuse, some sort of line between abusive and not abusive is required because professionals need a yardstick by which to decide whether to intervene or not. The following factors may influence where the line is drawn at any particular point in time:

- what is legal
- the effect on the child's well-being
- current beliefs about parenting practices
- current debates and issues relating to child abuse
- professional concerns
- the type of abuse.

Current child care and criminal law will give guidelines as to what is and is not abusive although definitions within the law can be difficult to interpret sometimes. However, in some areas the law is quite clear, for example, in giving age limits for sexual intercourse with female children. The effect on the child's well-being is likely to be related to the extent and duration of the abuse. Children may be seen to suffer few effects from one-off incidents of abuse, but abuse that is long term and chronic may be seen in a different light. For example, the child protection process may ignore a small bruise on a child's face if it occurs as an isolated incident. A similar small bruise on another child with a history of injuries may result in a much greater response. However, single incidents of sexual abuse can have longer-term effects and so may trigger the child protection process in a way that single incidents of physical abuse might not. Sexual abuse is generally found to be more easy to define than other forms of abuse. Perhaps this is because there is a clearer understanding in society of when a sexual act is considered to be abusive or not in relation to a child (Messages from Research, 1995, p. 19).

Why Are Children Abused?

Perhaps one of the most difficult adjustments that we may have to make when working with children is to learn to believe that abuse actually does take place. It can seem almost impossible that those responsible for caring for young children should purposefully inflict damage of a physical or psychological nature on their charges. However, in order to be able to contribute to the protection of the children in your care, it is necessary that you believe that child abuse can and does take place. Often child abuse that continues unchecked does so because the adults involved with the child fail to 'see' the abuse because they simply do not consider it as a possibility. Exploring the potential reasons why child abuse takes place may help to increase understanding about what child abuse is and how it can be prevented.

There are a number of different and sometimes conflicting theories about the causes of abuse. No theory can simply explain the complex nature of child abuse, but the following theories might offer some clues as to why children are abused. However, it should be remembered that these theories are based on studies of families which come to the attention of the child protection agencies, i.e. social services departments. These are much more likely to be poorer working-class families. Middle-class families who abuse are much less likely to become involved in the child protection process so much less is known about them.

Individual Theories

It is often thought that those who abuse children must be in some way different from the rest of the population, i.e. that they must be distorted, evil people who are in some way abnormal. A common reaction to newspaper or television reports about abuse is that the person 'must be sick to do such a thing'. In fact, it was once believed that all child abusers were psychopaths. However, we now know that child abuse is too widespread to be so easily explained. There are dangers in explaining all child abuse in this way as well. If we believe that child abuse is only committed by 'abnormal' people then we may be unable to recognize when a child is being abused by parents who are perceived as 'normal'.

Child abusers come from all walks of life, and are all sorts of people. However, despite this you may well ask why in certain circumstances some adults will abuse a child and others would not. The answers are complex and in some ways unclear. Research into child abuse has shown that certain characteristics and experiences may predispose particular individuals to be more likely to abuse a child in their care than another individual. These include:

- poor experiences of their own parenting which have resulted in low self-esteem and unmet needs dating from childhood
- mental health problems
- physical health problems
- a history of alcohol or drug abuse
- an unwanted pregnancy and/or a difficult birth
- unstable relationship with their partner
- becoming parents when still young
- poverty, poor housing and social isolation
- unrealistic expectations of the child.

It is essential to remember that the presence of one or more of these factors does not in itself indicate that child abuse will take place. However, many parents who abuse their children do share some or all of these characteristics, and clearly there is a link between the existence of these characteristics and an increased risk of child abuse taking place. Whether this increased risk actually results in abuse may well depend also on the social factors discussed below. There are no prescriptions for detecting that child abuse will take place in any particular family, but it may be that these factors can be taken in conjunction with other information to help identify the vulnerable families who may need support.

Family Dysfunction Theories

Another theory which looks at the family is the concept of family dysfunction. In families which dysfunction there are poor or distorted relationships between family members which result in inappropriate parenting. Often the dysfunction relates to the relationship between the adult partners. The relationship with the child may be influenced by this and the child may be used as a 'scapegoat' for all the family problems. In some cases the child may be unwanted, resulting in one or both of the adult partners feeling trapped and resentful in the family situation. This theory has been widely applied to explain child sexual abuse, particularly where children have been abused by their fathers. It has been much criticized by feminists who argue that the blame for sexual abuse is often placed on the mother or even the child as well as the father.

Sociological Theories

As well as theories which emphasize individual problems there are also theories which focus on social environments in which child abuse is more likely to take place. These sociological theories link child abuse with poverty and social deprivation including:

- poor housing, overcrowding and lack of amenities
- unemployment
- inadequate income, financial worries
- educational disadvantage.

Once again, none of these factors in itself will 'cause' abuse to take place. However, economic and social deprivation in an unequal society can add to the stresses and pressures experienced by some individuals and families, and this may in some cases increase the chances of child abuse taking place. It is important to remember, however, that child abuse can also take place in well-off and middle-class families, and that we should be careful not to create stereotypes of abusing families which focus on less well-off sections of society.

You have probably realized that individual and social factors cannot easily be separated from each other and that these factors are intertwined and mutually reinforcing. Child abuse takes place because of complex sets of interlinked social and personal factors affecting adults and children alike.

Feminist Theories

There is another possible explanation for the causes of child abuse, which has mainly been linked to child sexual abuse but which may have significance for other forms of abuse. These explanations focus on the imbalances of power in our society and the fact that children actually possess no rights as individuals within that society. One of the imbalances of power is between men and women. Some feminists would explain the sexual abuse of children as being a result of the fact that men possess the majority of power in our society and that this power is sometimes abused. Certainly other groups of people who suffer abuse in our society tend to be those who hold less power and have less say in the way society is organized, such as older people, disabled people and women. In the end, however, children who are sexually abused are abused for the sexual gratification of the adult – the fact that children are relatively powerless means that they have few means of preventing the abuse happening.

The issue of children's rights has been debated for a number of years and relates to the need to recognize that children often bear the brunt of poverty, inequality and deprivation in our society. For example, rising unemployment results in increased numbers of children living in poverty, which affects their health and welfare adversely. World-wide, children suffer from starvation and the effects of war. Children do not have a say in how their society operates, but are often affected by social and economic policies.

In some individual cases, social workers and other professionals have sometimes been criticized for not listening to the child's wishes and feelings about her circumstances, sometimes with tragic results. The 1989 Children Act emphasizes the need to ascertain the child's wishes and feelings and to incorporate the child's view as part of the criteria for decision-making about all aspects of her life. The child must also be the focus of the work and his welfare should be the most important aspect of any child protection processes which take place. Basically, this means that although professionals working with children may make every effort to help and support parents, their primary task is with the child. One of the criticisms aimed at social workers supervising the Care Order on Jasmine

Beckford, who was killed by her stepfather in 1984, was that they focused their time and energy on the parents not the child, and so Jasmine's ordeal of long-term abuse went unnoticed (DHSS, 1985). The issue of children's rights will be explored more fully in Chapter 7.

Children Who Are Abused

As well as trying to identify why certain adults abuse children, researchers have tried to identify why certain children are abused, i.e. whether abused children share a set of characteristics which may identify them. There are a number of factors which are more likely to be present in children who are abused than in children who are not abused. Like all these findings from research, the presence of one or more factors should not be considered as evidence that abuse will take place. They can only indicate likelihoods which may help professionals target support of particular families. Children who have been abused are more likely to share the following characteristics than other children:

- low birth weight
- abnormal pregnancy or birth
- illness of mother or child in the first year
- separation of child and parents after birth
- sleeplessness
- feeding problems
- persistent crying
- physical or learning disability.

We can never be sure why a particular child may be abused by a particular adult at any one point in time. It is probable that any number of different and complex factors come together to create the conditions in which abuse will take place. These will probably include social and environmental factors, as well as personal factors relating to the abuser. Only a small number of abusers suffer from major psychiatric or personality disorders. Research into the causes of child abuse needs to be treated with caution to avoid using the findings to stereotype certain groups of people as possible child abusers. However, the indicators described can be used in a positive way to ensure that more vulnerable children and families get the support and help they need in order to parent well.

≡ ❚❚ *Facts*

1. By the end of March 1994, there were 34,900 children's names on child protection registers.

2. This involved 31.7 children in every 10,000 children in the population.

3. In that year 28,500 children's names were added to the register and 26,200 were taken off after re-registration.

4. This involved an overall 7 per cent growth of numbers of names on the register.

5. 69 per cent of the children whose names were on the register were under 10 years old.

6. 40 per cent of new registrations related to children who were physically at risk, 25 per cent to those at risk of sexual abuse and 25 per cent at risk of neglect.

7. 55 per cent of those registered under the category of physical abuse were boys.

8. 62 per cent of those registered under the category of sexual abuse were girls.

9. 84 per cent of registrations during the year were registrations for the first time ever.

10. Children under 1 year old had the highest rate of registrations at 62.4 per 10,000 in the population.

The Facts about Child Abuse

The exact extent of child abuse in any society is difficult to establish because there are so many different ways of measuring what abuse is. Some definitions will include types of child abuse which other definitions exclude. In addition, not all child abuse is recognized and reported – some abuse never comes to light. This means that estimates of the extent or prevalence of child abuse should always be treated cautiously. Many of the figures come from official sources and deal with child abuse cases which have entered the child protection system. Therefore, these figures only represent the number of child protection cases which have been officially recognized. They may well exclude any number of cases where the child abuse was unrecorded or not seen as abusive by the criteria being used at the time.

Despite these reservations about their accuracy, child abuse statistics can be helpful in obtaining a picture of the extent and range of such abuse at any one time and to identify the increases and decreases in the amount of child abuse over time.

The Department of Health (DoH) gathers figures from local authority social services departments and publishes them annually. Many of these figures relate to numbers of children whose names have been placed on child protection registers. These registers are used to record concerns about children where abuse is believed to have taken place. The decision to place the child's name on the child protection register is taken at a case conference which is part of the child protection procedures in any local authority (see Chapter 4 for details). In the 1994 report on numbers of children on child protection registers the figures opposite were given.

We need to interpret what these figures mean a little more closely. The figures show an overall growth in numbers of children on the register. This represents a real growth in numbers of children registered because the previous year there were only 29.6 children per 10,000 in the population registered whereas by March 1994 there were 31.7 children per 10,000 registered. It is clear from the statistics that younger children are seen as being in more need of child protection, particularly those under 1 year old.

These statistics also show that:

- 30 per cent of the children on the register were registered under the category of neglect
- 37 per cent physical injury
- 28 per cent sexual abuse
- 13 per cent emotional abuse
- 2 per cent other categories.

These figures do not necessarily reflect the extent of different types of abuse. Children may be subject to more than one form of abuse but are only registered under one category. For example, the figures for emotional abuse will not reflect the long-term emotional harm experienced by children who have been sexually abused.

These figures cannot tell us the true extent of child abuse in our society. What they can tell us is the number of children who are subject to official concern as regards child abuse. They also show the trends in levels of that concern and how that concern is broken down by age and gender.

Research from the Thomas Coram Unit shows that 16 per cent of children have been beaten, 10 per cent hit on the head and 5 per cent kicked by their mothers. Smith found 14 per cent of children to have had experience of severe punishment (Smith *et al.*, 1995).

The NSPCC estimates that every year between 150 and 200 children are killed by their parents.

Being Aware of Child Abuse

The first step in developing skills in child protection is to become aware of child abuse. This involves becoming aware that child abuse does not just happen in rare isolated incidents but is relatively widespread. We also need to be aware that child abuse happens in all social and cultural groups, not just in families with difficulties. Disabled children may be particularly vulnerable to abuse. Awareness does not mean seeing every child as an abuse victim. It does mean bearing abuse in mind as a possible explanation for certain signs and symptoms an individual child may present. It does mean recognizing that 'nice' people and people we know may abuse. It also means that we are prepared to work on creating a non-abusive environment for the children we care for.

Professionalism in Child Protection

Previously in the chapter the way in which child abuse may affect our feelings was discussed. Feelings about the abuse of children can be very powerful, and feelings about child abusers can be very negative. As a private individual you may wish to express these feelings openly, but as a childcare worker this may not be the best way of helping the child. Many children love and are attached to parents that others view as inadequate if not abusive. Many children would opt to stay with abusive parents rather than move in with strangers. Condemning the parents does not help the child protection process because such condemnation may alienate all the family. Working with children who may have been abused can be enormously stressful for those involved. It is important that you develop support networks among colleagues or organizations you belong to in order to obtain help dealing with your feelings.

Conclusions

In this introductory chapter we have explored the concept of child abuse, and have determined that it is not fixed but is dependent on the social and cultural context it is being applied to. This means that there is no clear-cut line between abusive and non-abusive behaviour towards children. There will always be an area of uncertainty where behaviour could be interpreted as abusive or not. Similarly, there is no single set of reasons why child abuse takes place in particular families. Child abuse is a widespread phenomenon which affects all societies in the present and throughout history. Protecting children from abuse is dependent on your ability to recognize that child abuse does happen in all parts of society and could happen to the children you work with.

References

Dartington Social Research Unit (Bullock, R., Little, M., Millham, S. and Mount, K. (hereafter DSRU)) (1995) *Child Protection: Messages from Research*, London, HMSO, p. 12.

DHSS (1985) *A Child in Trust; Jasmine Beckford* (The Jasmine Beckford Report), London, HMSO.

DHSS (1987) *Whose Child?* (The Tyra Henry Report), London, HMSO.

Smith, M., Bee, P., Heverin, A. and Nobes, G. (1995) 'Parental Control within the Family: The Nature and Extent of Parental Violence to Children', in DSRU, *Child Protection: Messages from Research*, London, HMSO, p. 23.

Smith, M. and Grocke, M. (1995) 'Normal Family Sexuality and Sexual Knowledge in Children', in DSRU, *Child Protection: Messages from Research*, London, HMSO, p. 12.

Stainton Rogers, W., Hevey, D. and Ash, E. (1989) *Child Abuse and Neglect*, London, B.T. Batsford.

2

Types of Abuse

Introduction

In Chapter 1 the meaning of 'child abuse' and the difficulties of determining what is and is not abusive were explored. In this chapter different definitions of abuse will be examined and their usefulness assessed. The problems of defining child abuse and the way in which different definitions influence the measurement of child abuse will be discussed. It is common practice when writing about child abuse or discussing child abuse on a training course to categorize abuse into different types. In this chapter we will look at the different categories of abuse which are normally used and the limitations on the use of these categories. Much of this chapter is background reading for consideration and discussion to try and help you obtain an overall view of the different aspects of child abuse.

Definitions of Abuse: Limitations

If you have completed Exercise 1 in Chapter 1 you will have written your own definition of child abuse and compared it with that of a friend. You might find it helpful to try this exercise now if you have not already done so.

There is no single definition of child abuse which all those involved in working with abused children would agree on. Definitions have been formulated by the Department of Health, by the NSPCC, by researchers and writers and by the legal system. In Chapter 1 the notion of child abuse as a concept which changed over time and between societies was considered. In the same way, definitions of child abuse also alter over time in order to keep pace with changing perceptions of what child abuse is. Some researchers argue that it is not helpful to try and define child abuse at all because it is such a complex concept. They argue that such definitions can provide too rigid a concept of what child abuse is and exclude some areas of possible abuse. So, definitions can be useful as a means of helping us decide what is and what is not child abuse, but they should not be seen as a 'strait-jacket' on our perception of whether a particular child is suffering harm.

Definitions can be useful also for comparing research findings and gathering statistics on the incidence of child abuse. Research findings on different aspects of child abuse can be confusingly contradictory unless the differences in the definitions of child abuse used by the various researchers are made clear. Similarly, the prevalence of child abuse cases found through research will depend very much on what definition of child abuse was used as a measure. A broad definition of child abuse will mean many more children are considered to be abused than if the definition used is narrower.

Definitions of Child Abuse

One of the more general definitions of child abuse commonly quoted is Gilmour's. Gilmour argued that the fact that there are many differing definitions of child abuse shows that there is no single adequate definition. Gilmour defines child abuse in the broadest sense in the following way: 'Child abuse occurs when any avoidable act, or avoidable failure to act adversely affects the physical, mental or emotional well-being of a child' (Gilmour, 1988, p. 11). This very broad definition is problematic in that it probably defines all children as abused at some stage of their lives. If you think of children you know, then it is probably fairly easy to think of examples of when they were 'abused' within this definition. The concept of 'avoidable harm' covers acts which may not be deliberate but did not need to happen, e.g. bruising to a child's arms through rough handling during dressing.

Gil's definition is also general, and rather complex, but it is useful in that it recognizes that not all child abuse is the result of the acts of individuals. Gil defines child abuse as:

> Any act of commission or omission by individuals, institutions or society as a whole, and any conditions resulting from such acts or inaction, which deprive children of equal rights and liberties, and/or interfere with their optimal development, constitute by definition abusive or neglectful acts or conditions. (Gil, 1975, pp. 346–54)

Gil's definition introduces the idea of child abuse at societal level and the concept of equal rights for children. It is useful in reminding us that child abuse is a broad concept and that although we tend to deal with child abuse at an individual level, many children are abused by war, economic and political decisions, oppressive regimes and poverty.

A Chance to Think

 The concept of children's rights will be covered more fully in later chapters, but it is worth considering now how children may be abused by the societies they live in. Children are often much more vulnerable to the consequences of poverty, famine and war than are adults, probably because children are almost entirely powerless in most cultures and because they are dependent on adults for their most basic needs to be met.

Exercise 1

When you are reading, watching or listening to the news over the next few days, try and note examples of situations in which children are suffering because of events within the society they live in. Are they more affected by events than the adults in the same situation? Is there any official recognition of the specific problems children face in this situation? What sort of support is being offered and from whom? Consider your findings in relation to the knowledge you have of child abuse by individuals and the definitions of abuse in this chapter. Do you consider the children in your examples to be abused? If so, by whom? If possible, try to discuss these issues with a colleague or friend.

The Prevalence of Child Abuse

The prevalence of child abuse is difficult to establish because the figures will depend on the type of definition that is used, and the use of statistics on reported incidents of child abuse which may not reflect the true level. There is general agreement that child abuse cases are significantly under-reported. Some research is aimed at estimating the extent of child abuse whether reported or not, but there are many difficulties in getting an accurate

☰ ▌ *Facts*

The current legal definition of child abuse is the concept of 'significant harm' described in the 1989 Children Act, the main piece of legislation used to protect children from abuse at this time. The term 'harm' is defined as meaning 'ill-treatment or the impairment of health and development'. 'Ill-treatment' includes non-physical ill-treatment and sexual abuse. However, the term 'ill-treatment' is not defined in any precise way and the term 'significant' is not defined at all. This leaves room for interpretations of the term 'significant harm' by the courts and those involved in the child protection process. In the majority of cases, this is not a problem, but occasionally it can result in legal disagreements in individual cases. The 1989 Children Act is discussed in detail in Chapter 5.

response to research in such a sensitive and painful area of human experience. As such, the figures must be treated cautiously. For example, the rise in reported cases of child sexual abuse in the 1980s did not necessarily reflect a rise in the number of cases, but they did illustrate the growing awareness of child sexual abuse among both professionals and the general public during that time. The figures also reflected increasing social concern about this type of abuse which made disclosure more feasible and which alerted professionals involved with children to the signs and symptoms. Perhaps the most important aspect of child abuse statistics is that they persuade us to recognize that child abuse does exist and that it is widespread and not confined to particular groups or classes of people.

The circumstances of 160,000 children a year are assessed under Section 47 of the Children Act, 1989, which gives local authorities the duty to investigate possible cases of child abuse. Of these child abuse enquiries 25 per cent are found to be unsubstantiated. The children who are investigated under Section 47 are not typical of either the general population or representative of all children who are abused:

- Over 33 per cent of the families investigated are lone-parent families.
- Over 50 per cent are dependent on income support.
- In 27 per cent of cases domestic violence was a factor.
- In another 13 per cent of cases mental illness featured.
- 65 per cent of the children were known to the social services already.
- 45 per cent had been subject to a previous investigation.

This does not mean that families with these characteristics are the only families in which child abuse takes place, but it does mean that families with disadvantages are more likely to come to the attention of the social services child protection system (Gibbons, Conroy and Bell, 1995).

Child Protection Registers (see Chapter 4 for details) can be used to assess the extent of child abuse because they reflect the number of children on whom official concerns are focused. They do not reflect the extent of abuse of children in general terms. There is a wide discrepancy between the numbers of children who are abused and the proportion of these children who come to the attention of the child protection services. In March 1994 there were approximately 34,900 children's names on Child Protection Registers in England and Wales (DoH, 1995). The figures for children registered on Child Protection Registers have fallen since the 1989 Children Act was implemented. This may be because the category for registration, 'grave concern', has been dropped. Children would be registered under this category when they did not fit into one of the other four. On the other hand, this fall in numbers may be due to better child protection work under the Children Act.

Of the children who are subject to investigation, only 4 per cent actually leave home and 70 per cent of children who are looked after are later reunited with their families (Hallett and Birchall, 1995). The implication of this is that the child protection process is successful. It is also reassuring for those who are concerned that if they report a possible case of abuse they will be responsible for a child going into care, to know that this is unlikely to be the case. However, Farmer and Owen (1995) found that 25 per cent of children are re-abused after having their names placed on the Child Protection Register for physical abuse. Other research found that 43 per cent of child sexual abuse cases were 'unsafe' nine months after registration (Sharland et al., 1995).

As well as general definitions of child abuse there are also a variety of definitions for the different types of child abuse. However, like the general definitions these categories also have limitations.

Limitations of Using Categories

Although it is common to categorize different types of child abuse under a variety of headings, it is important to note that very few children suffer from abuse which can be neatly 'pigeon-holed' into one particular type or another. For example, children who are physically and/or sexually abused usually experience emotional damage, such as loss of confidence and lowered self-esteem. Similarly, neglected children may often feel unloved and unwanted. Children who are sexually abused may be subject to physical attacks, and are often threatened and coerced into concealing or denying the abuse. Farmer and Owen's (1995) study showed that:

- In one-third of cases where the main concern was neglect there were also concerns about physical abuse.
- In one-fifth of cases where the main concern was physical abuse there were also concerns about neglect.
- In one-quarter of cases where the main concern was sexual abuse there were also concerns about neglect.
- In one-sixth of cases where the main concern was sexual abuse there were also concerns about physical abuse.
- In one-quarter of cases where the main concern was physical abuse there were also concerns about emotional abuse.

For most children who are abused, there are no dividing lines between the different types of abuse they are subjected to – it is all part of the same experience. Categories of abuse should therefore be treated with caution; more as a tool for understanding what abuse is, rather than as a diagnosis of the problems an individual child may be experiencing. The dangers of sticking rigidly to categories is that in doing this we may overlook the complex nature of child abuse and the real experience of an individual child.

However, categories can help us understand more about the range and types of abuse that children suffer. The four main categories of child abuse are described in *Working Together under the Children Act 1989* (DoH, 1991; to be replaced in late 1998 by new guidelines. *Working Together to Safeguard Children*) in order to help case conferences make decisions about whether a child's name should be placed on the Child Protection Register or not.

The categories that we will consider are:

- physical abuse
- emotional abuse
- sexual abuse
- neglect.

A case study is provided for each category of abuse.

Physical Abuse

Physical abuse of children happens when an adult or adults deliberately inflict injuries on a child or knowingly fail to prevent the child coming to physical harm. Physical abuse may involve the following:

- hitting, punching or beating the child
- kicking
- burning
- scalding
- beating with an object, e.g. a belt
- smothering or suffocating the child
- poisoning
- shaking the child violently
- scratching, pinching or twisting parts of the child's body
- grabbing, squeezing or crushing parts of the child's body
- throwing the child, e.g. on to a wall or floor
- throwing an object or objects at the child
- stabbing or cutting.

In *Working Together under the Children Act 1989* the category of physical abuse also includes what is known as Munchausen's syndrome by proxy. Munchausen's syndrome involves an individual fabricating or simulating illnesses and receiving unnecessary medical treatment, possibly including surgery, as a result. Munchausen's syndrome by proxy is where the parent fabricates or induces symptoms of illness in a child in order that the child should receive unnecessary medical treatment or intervention (DoH, 1991). A recent well-known example of Munchausen by proxy is that of the nurse Beverley Allitt, who was convicted of the murder of several children in her care.

Children who are physically abused may suffer a variety of injuries over long or short periods of time. There is evidence to show that children who have minor injuries inflicted on them may be at risk of further more severe injuries at a later date and, therefore, minor injuries should always be thoroughly investigated. Severe physical abuse of children may result in permanent damage or death. Children who are killed by their carers have usually been physically abused regularly over a period of time and may have suffered multiple injuries during that period. Most children who are killed by their parents suffer multiple injuries around the time of death although head injuries and internal injuries are most often the actual cause of death.

Some physical abuse of children is described as over-punishment. This occurs when a child is subject to physical punishment from a carer which then 'goes too far', resulting in injury. This may be the result of the carer losing their temper or being unable to control their behaviour. It may also result from an escalation of punishment whereby the punishments become more severe over time because the lesser punishments are considered ineffective. Other physical abuse of children may be part of elaborate rituals of punishment and humiliation. These may involve deliberate attempts to terrify the child with threats of punishment to come, or may involve random attacks on the child for ever-changing reasons in order that the child has no opportunity to avoid punishment by changing her behaviour. In these cases, in the long run the psychological damage is usually much worse than the physical damage.

There have been a number of child death inquiries since the late 1970s which have highlighted the fact that every year 150–200 children are killed by their parents. A child abuse inquiry tends to take place when the professional child protection services are involved with a child who dies, in order to try and establish the ways in which these services failed to protect the child and to make recommendations for future working practices or changes in the relevant legislation. The majority of inquiries focus on cases where the child is physically abused to the extent that he or she dies. Some of these inquiry reports have been highly influential in shaping child protection legislation, policy and practice. The inquiry into the death of Jasmine Beckford who died in 1984 at the age of 4 served to catalyse the growth of clearer and more efficient inter-agency co-operation and to highlight the need for social workers to fully recognize their role in monitoring children who have been abused.

Jasmine and her younger sister were made the subject of Care Orders after physical abuse had taken place. After a period in foster care the children were returned home to their parents for a 'fresh start'. At the time the Care Orders were made the court had expressed a hope that the children would eventually be rehabilitated to their parents. The return home seemed superficially successful, but in fact there was little contact between the social worker and the family, and a failure by the social worker to focus on the children when contact was made. In addition, the health visitor also rarely saw the children and Jasmine quickly ceased to attend the nursery at which she had been allocated a place. Poor communication between the professionals involved resulted in lack of co-ordination of this information which, when put together, creates a picture which should have alerted the social worker to possible dangers to the children. Jasmine had suffered repeated abuse over a period of time and her body showed evidence of old scars and fractures as well as the injuries which caused her death. Jasmine's stepfather was found responsible for her manslaughter. The report into Jasmine's death described the social workers involved with her as 'naïve beyond belief' in their approach to the family and their failure to recognize the risks (DHSS, 1985).

The inquiry into the death of Kimberley Carlisle criticized the child protection system which had failed to operate successfully in Kimberley's case. The social worker was criticized for reacting too little and too late and the health visitor was criticized for not monitoring the child's health condition. However, this case also influenced the inclusion of a 'child assessment' order in the 1989 Children Act in response to the difficulties the social worker had in trying to get Kimberley medically examined.

Kimberley died from a head injury which was the culmination of a lengthy period of physical abuse and neglect. The inquiry report concluded that 'Kimberley had been tortured and starved for many weeks before her death'. Like Jasmine, Kimberley had been in foster care for a period of time before being returned to her parents to die at the hands of her stepfather eight months later. At the time of her death the social worker had been trying to gain access to Kimberley and to have her medically examined (DHSS, 1987).

A Chance to Think

Child abuse inquiries are lengthy and expensive and extraordinarily stressful for those who have to give evidence. The process of calling for an inquiry has been criticized at times on the grounds that they use a lot of public money to reach conclusions that could be reached in a less elaborate way. However, child death inquiries have served to bring to public attention the reality of child physical abuse and the possible consequences for the child and also to make recommendations for improving child protection practices. The Children Act, 1989, addressed many of the issues raised by inquiry reports in the 1980s. These included the need for clear procedures involving all agencies, emphasizing the need for different professionals to have clear-cut roles and the means of co-operating fully with each other over individual cases. The need to carefully monitor children who have been abused is emphasized as is the need to have a careful assessment of the risk to the child.

 Exercise 2

Read the case study below. Imagine that you are the nursery nurse responsible for Hannah. Write a list of all the factors you should consider when monitoring Hannah in the future. Obviously, your list would include observation of Hannah's physical condition, but what other aspects would cause you concern? Compare your answers with the sample answers in Appendix II.

Case Study of Physical Abuse

Hannah was 18 months old when she came to playgroup with bruising around her mouth. The bruises looked as if her face had been grasped over the mouth with considerable force. The playgroup was organized by two social workers who noticed the bruising and asked Gail, the mother, about it. Gail denied all knowledge of the bruising but later admitted that her new fiancé had squeezed Hannah's face to try and stop her crying. The case conference agreed that Hannah was not safe to live with her mother's fiancé after the paediatrician noted that other bruises had been found on Hannah's body. The fiancé was later prosecuted and imprisoned for 4 months for assault. Gail moved in with another man in the meanwhile. Nursery staff monitoring Hannah's progress alerted social workers to her lengthy absence from nursery. On investigation, Hannah was found to have a black eye, torn lip and bruising across her face. On this occasion, Hannah was taken into care although she was later successfully rehabilitated to her mother's care.

Emotional Abuse

Emotional abuse involves harm to the child's psychological and emotional development due to persistent and severe emotional ill-treatment. Emotional abuse can include:

- verbal abuse
- rejection and withdrawal of affection
- lack of warmth and physical contact, e.g. hugs
- constant criticism
- holding the child in poor regard
- telling the child repeatedly that he is unloved, unwanted and unacceptable
- telling others of the child's failings and shortcomings

- treating the child as less valuable or important than other children in the family
- ignoring the child, not communicating with him
- denying the child's achievements
- scapegoating the child, e.g. blaming her for other children's behaviour or acts
- threatening the child
- ridiculing the child.

There are a number of different definitions of emotional abuse which reflect professional confusion as to how to define the limits of emotional abuse. *Working Together under the Children Act 1989* does not give a clear definition of emotional abuse. It is possible that perfectly reasonable parents may occasionally respond to their child in some of the ways described above. However, emotional abuse occurs when children are subject to a constant barrage of emotionally damaging adult behaviour, not because of isolated incidents. This means that in order to be described as emotional abuse the behaviour must be severe and it must result in long-term damage to the child's emotional development.

Garbarino, Gutman and Seeley offer the following definition:

> A concerted attack on a child's development of self and social competence, a pattern of psychically destructive behaviour which consists of five forms: (1) rejecting (the adult refusing to acknowledge the child's worth and the legitimacy of the child's needs); (2) isolating (cutting the child off from normal social experiences, preventing the child from forming friendships, and making the child believe that he or she is alone in the world); (3) terrorising the child (verbal assault, creating a climate of fear, bullying and frightening a child, making the child believe that the world is capricious and hostile); (4) ignoring (depriving the child of essential stimulation and responsiveness, stifling emotional growth and intellectual development); (5) corrupting (stimulating the child to engage in anti-social behaviour, reinforcing that deviance, making the child unfit for normal social experience. (Garbarino, Guttman and Seeley, 1986, p. 12)

It is worth reflecting on this definition for a few minutes and considering what these outcomes of emotional abuse would mean to the child, in terms of her growth and development, her ability to learn and to enjoy the world around her, her chances of making affectionate and rewarding relationships and achieving a positive, constructive and contented adult lifestyle.

The above definition focuses on the outcomes for the emotionally abused child rather than the behaviour of the abusing parents. This approach is helpful in recognizing that there are many and varied types of adult behaviour towards a child which can result in emotional impairment. Rather than list all of these types of behaviour (probably an impossible task) the definition attempts to categorize the results of adult emotionally abusive behaviour whatever form it takes. As much emotional abuse of children actually results from other forms of abuse, this approach can help to keep the focus of the work with the child on the emotional impairment she has suffered.

Even for non-abused children, unfair criticism or ridicule and rejection can be painful and demoralizing for a period of time. Think back to your own childhood. Can you remember now incidents that left you feeling exposed and ashamed? These might include being laughed at, or treated with contempt or made to feel unwanted. Children can be highly sensitive to criticism and even minor incidents can have a short-term effect on the child's self-confidence. However, emotional abuse involves longer-term damage to the child's self-esteem and sense of self-worth which may leave the child with permanent emotional and psychological problems. These can include anxiety, nervousness, aggressive or withdrawn behaviour and an inability to participate in childhood activities and experience enjoyment.

If emotional abuse continues for a long period, the child may grow to adulthood struggling with depression or neurosis or even suicidal thoughts and acts. Emotional abuse usually results from other types of abuse, but can be treated as a separate category when it is the main form of abuse. It is, however, important to remember that where the child suffers from other types of abuse, it is often the attendant emotional damage that causes the long-term problems. For example, many sexually abused children do not suffer major physical injuries from the sexual abuse but the emotional effects of such abuse can last a lifetime. Similarly, adults who have suffered physical abuse as children will often continue to suffer the effects of that abuse long after the bones have mended and the scars have healed. Dealing with the emotional aspects of abuse is often the central theme when working with children who have been abused.

A Chance to Think

Emotional abuse can be difficult to prove in court. Expert witnesses such as clinical psychologists are often called in to assess the child's emotional and psychological state and then to give evidence in court. There is no crime of emotional abuse of a child, but emotionally abused children can be made subject to care proceedings under the 1989 Children Act if the child is suffering or likely to suffer 'significant harm' because of parental behaviour.

Exercise 3

Read the case study below. Try and write down some of the problems Gary's foster carers may have experienced when Gary was first placed with them. What long-term problems might a child like Gary experience? For example, Gary might find it difficult to make sense of his early experience because his learning difficulties may make communication hard for him. Compare your answers with the sample answers in Appendix II.

Case Study of Emotional Abuse

Gary was the second of five children. He lived with both parents. Gary was born with brain damage which resulted in learning difficulties and some behavioural problems. He was left alone for long periods of time as his parents refused to take him out, and he was tied to a chair and ignored for large parts of the day. His brothers and sisters were encouraged to verbally abuse Gary and to tease him until he became upset. Then his parents would scream abuse at Gary and tell him they wished he was dead. His mother said she hated Gary and did not want him in the house. In the end, Gary was removed to residential care and later fostered with a family. His parents refused to see him again. Gary displayed some very difficult behaviour when he first went into care, being aggressive and destructive and having frequent violent tantrums. He was assessed at a specialist hospital unit to determine how best to help him, and eventually Gary responded to the care he received and to the efforts of the staff at the special school he attended. Gary was eventually seen as ready to live with a family again, and after a rather difficult start he settled well with his foster carers, and learned to love and trust them. Gary was probably helped by having good quality care and experienced foster carers, and because he was relatively young when he was removed from the abusive situation.

Sexual Abuse

Sexual abuse of children involves any sexual behaviour or activity through which an adult uses a child for his or her own sexual gratification. The child may be forced or coerced into the sexual activity and may be too immature to fully understand the nature of the activities in which he has been involved. The child may be bribed or threatened to prevent him disclosing the abuse. The child may also be persuaded into the sexual activity if it appears to be the main way in which the parent will show him any apparent affection. The NSPCC suggests the following definition of child sexual abuse:

> Any child below the age of consent may be deemed to have been sexually abused when a sexually mature person has, by design or by neglect of their usual societal or specific responsibilities in relation to the child, engaged or permitted the engagement of that child in any activity of a sexual nature which is intended to lead to the sexual gratification of the sexually mature person. This definition would apply whether or not this activity involves explicit coercion by any means, whether or not there is discernible harmful outcome in the short-term. (Marchant and Page, 1992)

Sexual abuse of children could include the following:

- sexual intercourse including vaginal or anal penetration
- rape
- masturbation of the child or of the adult by the child
- oral sex with the child or by the child
- touching, fondling or kissing the child in a sexual manner and for sexual gratification
- child pornography involving the inclusion of children in sexual activities with other adults or each other, possibly animals or objects and recording these activities on video, film or still photographs which can be sold or otherwise distributed
- child prostitution which would involve the child in sexual activity with a number of partners who pay
- showing the child pornographic material in order to sexually stimulate the child
- involving the child in sexual activities with other adults and children for the sexual gratification of the adults present
- indecent exposure.

Definitions of child sexual abuse sometimes contain references to 'informed consent' and to the child's developmental inability to truly comprehend the acts which they were involved in. It is clear that children are not able to give consent as would an adult because of the power differences between an adult and child. Children are essentially dependent on adults and do not have the same choices about relationships as do adults. One 8-year-old girl who had been raped by her stepfather said that she had agreed to some of the earlier sexual molestation because she was afraid and because 'he was her father' and as such had authority over her. She had not known what the activities would be and had no concept of how to refuse her stepfather's wishes. The question of 'informed consent' seems superfluous in a situation where the child has so little control over events. However, paedophile groups argue that children can give informed consent to sexual activities and as such the adult would not be guilty of a misdeed if he or she involved the child in such activities.

The incidence of child sexual abuse is often considered to be greater than available statistics may indicate. There is a big difference between the statistics for reported sexual abuse and estimates of the real level of sexual abuse in Britain and other countries. Child sexual abuse may go unreported for years, or may only come to light when the child becomes an adult. Researchers often have to use adult respondents to try and get figures for the incidence of child sexual abuse, so there is a time-lapse between when the abuse took place and the gathering of data about the abuse, which may affect the quality of the outcomes. Statistics of successful prosecutions imply low rates because of the difficulties of successfully prosecuting child sexual abuse cases.

However, sexual abuse in Britain is seen as affecting up to one in eight girls and one in twelve boys. Some researchers put the estimate as high as one in four girls. Obviously the figures depend on what definition of child sexual abuse is used. The figures will be lower if the less damaging types of sexual abuse are excluded. Kelly, Regan and Burton used a sample of 1,244 16–21-year-olds to establish how many had had unwanted sexual experiences. They drew up a scale of nine definitions of sexual abuse in increasing severity. The widest definition found 60 per cent of women and 25 per cent of men had been subject to some unwanted sexual attention. By the strictest definition 4 per cent of women and 2 per cent of men had been sexually abused. The rates fell noticeably when the definition changed to include physical contact (Kelly, Regan and Burton, 1991). It may be worthwhile to pause here for a moment and consider what you would include in a definition of sexual abuse. Would you include comments, gestures, jokes or exposure to sexual images? Or would you only include activities that involved physical contact? Think about the sorts of activities that you personally would find unacceptable in terms of sexual behaviour. Try and think of examples of behaviour towards children or images of children which you feel are unacceptable because of their sexual content.

Child sexual abuse can occur within or outside the family. It was once believed that children were mainly sexually abused by strangers. Nowadays there is widespread acceptance that children are sexually abused within families and that a large proportion of abusers are fathers and stepfathers. Other family members can also be involved, including grandfathers, brothers and uncles. Women also abuse children sexually but current figures report a low percentage of female sexual abusers compared to male sexual abusers. Most children are sexually abused by adults they know. Children are also sexually exploited outside the family in other ways. For example, child prostitution is widespread across the world and children are exploited to produce pornographic material in many countries.

Many feminists suggest that child sexual abuse is widespread rather than unusual in society. They argue that the majority of female children are subject to some form of sexual abuse from the males in their family during childhood and that this is part of a more general domination of females by males. However, this does not fully explain the number of boys subject to sexual abuse which may well be much higher than the figures suggest.

The figures for child sexual abuse have increased during the 1980s as recognition and open debate about child sexual abuse have created the opportunity for children and adults to disclose their own experiences. One woman aged 60 disclosed the sexual abuse she had suffered over 50 years ago after watching a programme on television about incest survivors. The experience was as fresh in her mind as if it had happened that week. She was astonished and profoundly relieved that her experience, which she had felt to be so disgraceful that she could never admit to it, was not only shared by others, but was now being sympathetically and sensitively received.

One of the more recent developments in the assessment of the extent of child sexual abuse in our society is the growing recognition that increasingly other children are involved in child sexual abuse. The National Children's Home (NCH) *Report of the Committee of Enquiry into Children who Sexually Abuse Other Children* (NCH, 1992) stated that one-third of child sexual abusers are themselves under 18 years old. Most of these are boys. There needs to be more research into why boys sexually abuse other children as it is not clear why this happens. One theory is that the boys who sexually abuse others may have been sexually abused themselves.

Disabled children may be particularly vulnerable to sexual abuse. They may be more isolated with fewer contacts outside the family, or it may be that the adults involved with the disabled child may not recognize the signs of sexual abuse because they assume the signs and symptoms of the abuse are related to the child's disability. Some children may not be able to disclose what has happened to them because they have limited ability to communicate. Disabled children may not be able to comprehend or carry out self-help strategies to protect themselves from abuse (see Chapter 7). Disabled children may also be less likely to be believed by adults when they try to disclose sexual abuse. Sadly, disabled children in residential and day care may be vulnerable to sexual abuse, perhaps because abusers feel that such children may find it difficult to disclose what has happened to them.

Stereotypes of black and Asian families may prevent children in these families from being protected from sexual abuse. Assumptions and confusions about non-white cultures may mislead white professionals who are involved with those families. Black and Asian children may find it harder to develop relationships of trust with white childcare workers within which they could disclose abuse. Finally, fears of being seen as racist may prevent white childcare workers from looking into their concerns about a black or Asian child more closely.

There are a number of pieces of legislation which make the sexual exploitation of children a criminal offence. However, there are areas where the issue of whether a particular event is sexually abusive or not is less clear. These usually relate to teenagers who may be having sex with others of their own or a similar age. Although these activities may be illegal they may not be regarded as sexually abusive.

Not all children who are sexually abused by adults are forced or attacked. Although some children are subject to dreadful assaults involving physical damage and trauma, other children are subject to more subtle attacks which may involve a gradual process within which the child is introduced to various types of sexual activity without any assault or physical coercion. The child may suffer little physical pain and may not be initially greatly traumatized by the events. However, as children mature they come to realize that the activities which they are involved in are considered morally wrong and this may result in great emotional distress. Many children suffer from guilt for letting the abuse happen or for enjoying some of the aspects of the abuse, despite the fact that they clearly had no choice in the matter.

Child pornography is usually organized by a number of adults and can involve very young children. In one case young children aged between 1 and 8 were being used to simulate sexual activities with adults in order that pornographic videos could be made. Although the sexual activities were simulated the children all suffered long-term emotional damage, particularly the 8-year-old who was sexually stimulated by the activities and had to deal with the guilt he felt about this.

Although there are clearly stated offences within the law which relate to the sexual abuse of children, in fact many abusers are not prosecuted because sexual abuse can be difficult to prove. Medical evidence may not exist or it may prove inconclusive, e.g. if there is evidence that the child has suffered vaginal penetration but there is no evidence as to who was responsible for this abuse. Perpetrators have strong incentives to conceal and deny their activities not only because of the likelihood of prosecution, but because of the social condemnation to which child sexual abusers are subject. Child sexual abuse breaks fundamental taboos and can produce violent reactions in members of the public.

Convicted child sexual abusers frequently have to be protected from other prisoners who may physically assault them.

The majority of child sexual abuse is an intensely secret process. Often only the abuser and the child know what has happened, and despite the increased levels of help children now get to give evidence in court, often it is the child's word against the adult's. The court experience may be far too distressing for certain children, and young children are not always considered able to give reliable evidence in court. Many children are never asked to give evidence because they are considered too emotionally fragile after the abuse to endure a further ordeal. Some children may be prepared for a court case but may lose confidence during the long period of time that it takes for the case to come to court. It is hard for sexually abused children sometimes to see their abuser go unpunished, but many do.

Child sexual abuse has been in the public eye increasingly through the 1980s (see Chapter 1) and the reported incidence of this type of abuse has risen dramatically in that time. Some believe that despite the increased recognition of child sexual abuse, many cases go unreported. In response to the increased recognition of child sexual abuse there has been the need for the development of professional and agency responses to that abuse. These have on occasion been severely criticized by various inquiry reports which have in turn been widely reported in the media. Perhaps the most well-known and controversial report is the Cleveland Report, which is the outcome of an inquiry into the way in which a large number of suspected child sexual abuse cases were handled in the Cleveland area. In this case, unlike the child death inquiry cases already discussed, the professionals involved were not criticized for failing to act to protect the children involved; instead they were criticized for taking actions which were considered excessive and inappropriate and which were based on controversial evidence (Butler-Sloss, 1988).

The Cleveland inquiry resulted from the complaints of a group of parents whose children had been taken into care because of suspected child sexual abuse. At the heart of the controversy was the use of the 'reflex anal dilation' test as a method of ascertaining whether sexual abuse had taken place or not. Children were deemed to have been sexually abused on the basis of medical evidence alone, some of which was notably controversial. The situation was made worse by an ever-increasing number of suspected cases, and the professional and personal disagreements between the hospital paediatricians and police surgeons. Parents were not allowed to see their children and were given little information about what was happening to them. Children were brought into care on Place of Safety Orders (the emergency Court Order used prior to the Children Act 1989 to bring children into care when they were in immediate danger) despite the fact that sexual abuse is usually not life-threatening. The result was that 121 children were deemed to be sexually abused over a five-month period resulting in total overload on the child protection system. In addition, although procedures and guidelines for inter-agency co-operation existed they were not always followed and there was hostility and disagreement between some of the professionals involved.

The report recommended better inter-agency co-operation and the need to assess the child's condition and situation fully before concluding that sexual abuse has taken place. Parents should be kept fully informed particularly about their rights, e.g. to contact with their children. The child's story should be listened to, but the child should not be subject to repeated interviews or medical examinations. The outcomes of the Cleveland Report for policy and practice were the establishment of improved methods of liaison between agencies, for example, joint training for police officers and social workers who investigate child sexual abuse; specialist units for investigating child sexual abuse involving professionals from different agencies; guidelines on working with parents. Many of these recommendations are outlined in the previously cited document, *Working Together under the Children Act 1989*, which gives explicit guidelines on how different child protection agencies should respond to child abuse and how liaison between agencies should be achieved.

A Chance to Think

It is often difficult to prove cases of sexual abuse in court and successfully convict the perpetrators. In the past, there have been problems between social workers and police officers because their different roles in a child sexual abuse case are sometimes incompatible. The police are looking for evidence that a crime has been committed, in order to bring charges against a specific individual or individuals, while the social workers have the job of protecting the child. Measures such as specialist units and joint training are designed to try and minimize any conflict between different professional interests, and to maximize the chances of protecting the child and prosecuting those responsible for the abuse.

 ## Exercise 4

Read the case study below. Why do you think Bob was not prosecuted? What sort of problems would there have been trying to prove that abuse had taken place in a court of law? Think about the sort of pressures that can be brought to bear on children to make them deny sexual abuse has taken place or retract disclosures that have already been made. Compare your answers to the sample answers in Appendix II.

Case Study of Sexual Abuse

Norman was 4 when his elder sister, Jane, then 10 years old, disclosed to her teacher that a family friend had been abusing her for several years. The children lived in an 'open house' and the friend, Bob, came and went as he pleased, often staying the night. Jane told the social workers that she had been touched on the genitals and made to touch Bob's penis. Bob had tried to have intercourse with Jane but had not succeeded. Jane told the social worker that Bob stayed in Norman's room when he stayed the night. The mother confirmed this, but said that nothing could have happened because Bob 'liked girls not boys'. Norman refused to talk about Bob for some weeks, but eventually disclosed abuse at nursery during a play session with the doll's house. Norman demonstrated to the nursery staff that a man got into his bed, touched his penis, and then penetrated him anally. He said this man was Bob. Medical evidence suggested that anal penetration had taken place. Bob was not prosecuted because the mother did not support the children's testimony, and eventually both children denied the abuse had taken place. The children were made the subjects of Care Orders.

Neglect

Neglect occurs when the child's parents fail to meet the child's basic needs, such as food, clothes, warmth and shelter, hygiene and medical care. The child may also be neglected through inadequate supervision such as when a young child is left alone or in charge of even younger children, or when a child is allowed to wander in the community without supervision or concern for his whereabouts. Essentially, neglect usually refers to not doing something to care for the child rather than actively harming the child as in physical abuse. Neglect can result from:

- inadequate or inappropriate food
- inadequate or inappropriate clothing
- denying or failing to provide the child with adequate warmth and shelter
- failing to wash or bath the child
- failing to provide the child with clean clothing and a hygienic environment

- not responding to the requirements of a child's developmental stage, e.g. not toilet-training the child
- failing to supervise the child in potentially dangerous situations where the child may be injured or killed, e.g. letting a toddler play near a busy road with no supervision
- failing to seek medical attention when the child is ill or injured.

Neglect refers to the persistent failure to meet a child's needs rather than one-off omissions in a normally adequate pattern of parenting. *Working Together under the Children Act 1989* defines neglect as:

> The persistent or severe neglect of a child, or the failure to protect a child from exposure to any kind of danger, including cold or starvation, or extreme failure to carry out important aspects of care, resulting in the significant impairment of the child's health or development, including non-organic failure to thrive. (DoH, 1991, p. 48)

'Non-organic failure to thrive' is the term used to describe a condition in which the child fails to develop adequately where no identifiable physical cause (such as an illness) can be found. Children who fail to thrive often do so because of a combination of physical and emotional neglect. The symptoms of failure to thrive may disappear rapidly when the child is moved to a more caring environment (see Chapter 3).

Neglected children are usually neglected in a number of ways and these may combine to increase the child's misery. For example, the child may be more likely to become ill or be injured through poor diet, inadequate clothing and poor supervision. If the parents do not seek medical attention for the child then illnesses can become acute or chronic. One young boy was sent out of the house to play from the age of 2 onwards and left out in cold, wet weather without a coat or jumper. He was poorly nourished and unable to keep himself warm. The boy suffered a series of ear infections which went untreated and which eventually resulted in permanent hearing impairment. The child was delayed in all aspects of growth and development and was frequently ill from childhood onwards.

Neglected children might not attend nursery or school because no one takes them there or they might go by themselves at too young an age. The child may arrive early in school and be reluctant to go home.

Like emotional abuse, neglect can be difficult to define accurately. Children growing up in households on low incomes may appear to be neglected, despite the efforts of their parents to provide adequately for them, because there may simply not be the resources to meet all the child's needs. Although neglect is often associated with poverty, children can be neglected in households where there is the potential to meet their needs. Neglect may result from parental indifference or a gross lack of knowledge of the needs of children or the mental illness or learning disability of the parent. For example, a 6-year-old girl was left by her father in the care of a woman with substantial learning disability. Despite good intentions the woman was unable to recognize the child's needs and meet them. On one occasion she spent the entire week's food money on strawberries because they looked and smelled attractive.

A Chance to Think

Standards of childcare vary considerably within and between different cultures. It can be difficult to arrive at a set of criteria for deciding whether a child has been neglected or not, and often different professionals have differing views on the subject of minimum acceptable levels of basic care. Children's growth charts can provide a lot of information about a child's physical development, but other factors such as illness have to be ruled out before neglect can be proved.

Exercise 5

Read the case study below. In what ways could the nursery staff have tried to help Harry's grandmother provide a better standard of care? What sort of support might she have needed? Have you considered the financial aspects of the situation? Compare your answers to the sample answers in Appendix II.

Case Study of Neglect

Harry was a mixed race child with a white mother and Asian father. The parents separated and later the mother married a white man. Susan, the mother, was ashamed of having what she called a 'Paki child' and when she had two other children in rapid succession she began to ignore Harry's existence. Harry went to live with his maternal grandmother. She refused to buy clothes for Harry, who was often found in thin cotton with no coat in the coldest weather. Harry was very undernourished – at nursery he would eat until he was sick if not stopped.

He usually had a runny nose and various minor ailments which never received treatment. Harry was often left at nursery, because his grandmother sent an odd assortment of people to fetch him, many who simply did not turn up. Harry was left with anyone who would have him for a few hours. He developed major problems with his teeth which literally rotted away causing infections and a great deal of pain. Harry eventually went into foster care when his grandmother died and thrived so well that he stayed there and was later adopted. By this time his mother had moved and refused point-blank to have him back.

Incidence of Different Types of Child Abuse

When child abuse was first 'discovered' (and this is a bit like Columbus 'discovering' America, in that those who already lived there already knew about it) in the 1960s, it was the incidence of child physical abuse that came to the attention of doctors and social workers, and eventually the public. The 'battered baby syndrome' as it was called, aroused strong feelings of disbelief and outrage among professionals and public alike. It has been clear since then that statistics about the amount of child abuse in a particular society at a particular time should be treated with caution. It is generally believed that all types of child abuse are consistently under-reported, for a wide variety of reasons, which we will explore later in this chapter.

However, physical abuse, by its very nature, is easier to detect than the other types. Some physical abuse will never come to light, or will go undetected for long periods of time but, in general, the recorded incidence of physical abuse is probably the most statistically accurate of all types.

On the other hand, the extent of neglect of children is much harder to prove, perhaps because it is more difficult to define what we see as neglectful. Although we would all say, for example, that depriving a child of food and water for several days is certainly abusive, there are other more debatable areas of neglect. For example, we may describe children sent to nursery in grubby, smelly clothes, as neglected. But, do we mean that they are abused? Statistics about neglect therefore, reflect somebody's view of what neglect actually is, and this may not be your view, or the view of the next person.

Emotional abuse is similarly difficult both to define and measure. As we discussed in Chapter 1, definitions of abuse are not fixed concepts – they vary according to time and place, in other words, they are culturally determined. So, in the 1990s we would probably consider many Victorian child-rearing practices as emotionally abusive, in that they are designed to control and diminish independent behaviour, and stultify exploration and free-thinking. However, some would argue in this day and age that sending young children to boarding-school could be considered emotionally abusive, in that these children are separated from their loved ones and sent to live with strangers. Could we also argue that parents who move from area to area seeking employment and a better standard of living are abusing their children with constant disruptions and separations? As we discussed before, there are no clear dividing lines to tell us what is and is not abusive, so we need to treat the statistics with caution and an understanding of their limitations.

Child sexual abuse has probably been the most controversial and difficult type of abuse to define and measure. Sexual abuse of children is probably much more common than the figures indicate, for a number of reasons. First, measuring child sexual abuse depends on what definitions are used to decide what is measured. For example, if a young child is made to watch pornographic videos so that an adult can gain sexual gratification from that child's response, many of us would consider this abusive. However, statistically, there is little to go on in situations where there has been no contact between adult and child, and there is no medical evidence available. Therefore, some types of sexual abuse are both hard to define, and hard to measure. Secondly, the concept of sexual abuse of children is largely horrifying to our society. This makes it very difficult for children to report, and can make it difficult for adults to recognize – it is too shocking, and so we do not want to see it or believe it. For many children the process of discussing the highly painful and intimate details of their sexual abuse can appear much more of an ordeal than allowing the abuse to continue. It is widely believed among professionals in this field that for boys in particular, there are high levels of under-reporting of sexual abuse. Perhaps this is because our society still attaches stigma to homosexual acts, and this creates another significant barrier to reporting.

Conclusions

Children are abused in many different ways in societies across the world. Definitions and categories of abuse can be helpful in trying to measure the extent of child abuse in a particular society at a particular time, but they do not always help us know what child abuse is. This can be more meaningfully judged by listening to the experience of the child. Measuring the extent of child abuse can be haphazard. There are so many factors which affect levels of reporting of child abuse that the figures cannot be expected to be accurate. It is commonly believed that all child abuse is consistently under-reported and that research only shows us the 'tip of the iceberg'. Perhaps the most important point is that child abuse is widespread and common across a range of classes, cultures and types of families, and that children often suffer unheard because this is not always recognized.

References

Butler-Sloss, E. (1988) *Report of the Committee of Enquiry into Child Abuse in Cleveland* (The Cleveland Report), London, HMSO.

DHSS (1985) *A Child in Trust; Jasmine Beckford* (The Jasmine Beckford Report), London, HMSO.

DHSS (1987) *A Child in Mind; Protection of Children in a Responsible Society* (The Kimberley Carlisle Report), London, HMSO.

DoH (1991) *Working Together under the Children Act 1989 – a Guide to Inter-agency Co-operation for the Protection of Children from Abuse*, London, HMSO. (To be replaced by *Working Together to Safeguard Children* in late 1998.)

DoH (1995) *Children and Young People on Child Protection Registers year Ending 31st March 1994 England*, London, Government Statistical Service.

Farmer, E. and Owen, M. (1995) 'Child Protection Practice: Private Risks and Public Remedies – Decision Making, Intervention and Outcome in Child Protection Work', in DSRU, *Child Protection: Messages from Research*, London, HMSO, pp. 61–4.

Garbarino, Guttman and Seeley (1986) *The Psychologically Battered Child: Strategies for Identification, Assessment and Intervention*, San Francisco, Jossey-Bass.

Gibbons, J., Conroy, S. and Bell, C. (1995) 'Operating the Child Protection System: A Study of Child Protection Practices in English Local Authorities', in DSRU, *Child Protection: Messages from Research*, London, HMSO, pp. 68–70.

Gil, D. (1975) 'Unravelling Child Abuse', *American Journal of Orthopsychiatry*, **45**, pp. 346–54.

Gilmour, A. (1988) *Innocent Victims: The Question of Child Abuse*, London, Joseph.

Hallett, C. (1995) 'Inter-agency Co-ordination in Child Protection' in DSRU, *Child Protection: Messages from Research*, London, HMSO.

Hallett, C. and Birchall, E. (1992) 'Co-ordination and Child Protection', in DSRU, *Child Protection: Messages from Research*, London, HMSO.

Kelly, L., Regan, L. and Burton S.(1991) '*An Exploratory Study of the Prevalence of Sexual Abuse in a Sample of 16–21 year olds*', Child and Woman Abuse Studies Unit, University of North London, in DSRU, *Child Protection: Messages from Research*, London, HMSO, pp. 88–9.

Marchant, R. and Page, M. (1992) *Bridging the Gap: Child Protection Work with Children with Multiple Disabilities*, London, NSPCC.

NCH (1992) *Report of the Committee of Enquiry into Children Who Sexually Abuse Other Children*, London, National Children's Homes.

Sharland, E., Jones, D., Aldgate, G., Seal, H. and Croucher, M. (1995) *Professional Intervention in Child Sexual Abuse*, London, HMSO.

3

Signs and Symptoms of Abuse

Introduction

Two of the questions most frequently asked during child protection training sessions are 'How can I tell the difference between abuse and accidental injury?' and 'How can I tell if a child is telling the truth or not?' Childcare workers often feel that it is an overwhelming responsibility to be in a situation where they may have to report abuse. Reporting abuse could result in conflict with parents, with senior staff and with colleagues. A report that results in no action being taken could be interpreted as malicious. Childcare workers can also fear for their own safety, for example, if an irate parent decides to blame them for bringing in an investigative team.

The many and varied reasons for not reporting abuse are dealt with in the next chapter, but at this stage it is important to remember that if suspicions of abuse are not reported, then a child may remain in pain and fear for much longer, resulting in long-term physical and psychological damage. Your ability to recognize and act on signs and symptoms of abuse depends on two things – first, your ability to interpret what you see and hear, and secondly, your belief that abuse can and does take place.

The most important message about recognizing abuse is that *your* responsibility is not to decide whether abuse has taken place or not – that is a job for the doctors and social workers – but to report concerns and suspicions to the appropriate person. The task of establishing the facts will be taken on by medical and social work staff, and possibly the police, working together in a multidisciplinary child protection team. So, you will not be expected to judge the information you have, but you will need to ensure that you fulfil your responsibilities by passing the information on. Although your involvement may not end at this stage, there will be qualified social workers, and possibly police officers, to conduct a full investigation. Ultimately, it is often the courts which will decide the child's future.

A Chance to Think

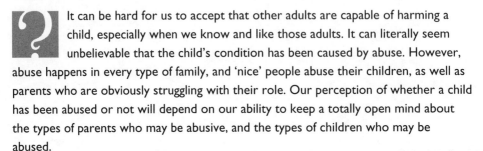

It can be hard for us to accept that other adults are capable of harming a child, especially when we know and like those adults. It can literally seem unbelievable that the child's condition has been caused by abuse. However, abuse happens in every type of family, and 'nice' people abuse their children, as well as parents who are obviously struggling with their role. Our perception of whether a child has been abused or not will depend on our ability to keep a totally open mind about the types of parents who may be abusive, and the types of children who may be abused.

 Exercise 1

1. Write down where you think that stereotypes of abusing families come from. Why are these stereotypes dangerous? Compare your answers with the sample answers in Appendix II.
2. Look at the four pictures of children in Figure 3.1. Which of these children do you think might be abused and why? Look at the sample answers in Appendix II.

The rest of this chapter is divided into four sections each of which explores the possible indicators for the different categories of abuse. There is some cross-over between indicators of the different types of abuse, especially behavioural indicators. Many children suffer different types of abuse at the same or different times in their lives, so the indicators may represent a complex pattern of abuse by one or more adults. Some types of abuse are difficult to detect if we rely on physical signs alone, but might be apparent in the child's behaviour. It is often impossible for a child to communicate in words what is happening to him. This may be simply because the child is too young to have the necessary language skills, or it could be that the child has been threatened and is too frightened to speak out. With sexual abuse in particular, the child might be ashamed and blame himself for what is happening to him, and this could prevent the child from speaking out. A child may

Leanna

Eddie

Peter

Susanna

Figure 3.1

communicate through behaviour when words are not possible, and the greater the child's feelings of pain and hurt, the more disturbing their behaviour could appear to others.

We need to remember that the child is reacting to what is happening to her, or using behaviour which she has learned from an adult, e.g. a child who is subject to physical violence may well be violent herself to other children.

Children with learning and physical disabilities might have developmental delays because of their disability. Be aware that children with disabilities are vulnerable to abuse, not the least because it may be difficult to recognize the signs and symptoms of abuse in a child where developmental delays or behavioural problems are already part of the child's character. Disabled children may be prone to small accidents, but this does not mean that all bruises on disabled children are accidentally caused. Use your knowledge of the child himself to help you ascertain any concerns about him.

We may also find it more difficult to recognize abuse in a child of a different culture from our own. Perhaps we have different expectations of children from different racial and cultural backgrounds or we may feel that we do not know what is 'normal' behaviour and appearance for this child. However, you do know the children in your care – use that knowledge and trust your own judgement. If you are not sure whether or not you have something to be concerned about, ask for advice from the 'appropriate person'. For example, you may not be used to a range of skin textures and colours and so you may need advice on whether the child is bruised or you are looking at normal variations in skin colour.

A Chance to Think

When we are having to manage the behaviour of children who are disruptive, aggressive, attention-seeking and difficult to control we can sometimes be overwhelmed by the task at hand, especially if care of a particular child absorbs a lot of time at the expense of other children. It can be easy to see such a child as 'naughty' and even 'bad'. We need to take time to reflect on the underlying causes of the child's behaviour, and to remind ourselves that happy, secure children do not usually behave in these ways. Whether the cause of the difficult behaviour is abuse or not, it is likely that the child has problems and fears with which he needs help.

Exercise 2

Write down a list of questions you might ask yourself and others, if a child in your care is behaving in difficult ways, or has become disruptive or aggressive. Compare your answers to the sample answers in Appendix II.

The indicators of abuse are many and varied, so in order to keep the lists fairly short, only the indicators that you might reasonably be expected to be aware of have been included. For example, a child may have healed fractures that indicate a history of physical abuse, but you would not normally be in a position to know this. However, you would be in a position to recognize that a child has pain in an arm or leg from a recent injury.

At each stage alternative explanations for the indicators are considered. Perhaps the most important thing to remember is that you *know* the children in your care, and you will know when they are different or unhappy or worried. It is this knowledge of the children who you care for which will help you to decide if there is a problem.

Finally, it is important to keep records of concerns. Isolated indicators of abuse can be meaningless, but patterns of changed behaviour, injuries or absences can build into a fairly clear picture of something being amiss. Children rarely present only one or two indicators of abuse. It is much more usual to see a number of changes, in the child's behaviour, manner, appearance, attendance and achievement at nursery or school, and general development.

Physical Abuse

How do we recognize a physical injury that has been inflicted by another person, when most children are covered with bumps and bruises from the day they start to walk? Many of you may worry about how we can tell the difference between accidental and inflicted injury. There are no certainties that you will always be able to tell. However, there are a number of factors that can help you decide whether a problem does exist for a particular child. One of these factors is to be aware of the most common sites of accidental injuries. When children fall, what do they fall on? Children usually damage themselves on their hands, knees and shins during falls, and on elbows, foreheads, noses and chins – in fact, all the bony bits. In addition bruising caused in accidents is usually to the front of the body. Our bodies are designed to protect the more vulnerable organs by surrounding them with bone. For example, eye sockets protect our eyes during a fall on the face.

Secondly, it is vital to take into account the child's age and developmental stage. This will tell you whether the injury is likely to have occurred to that particular child. For example, the scabby knees children seem to wear almost permanently after they learn to toddle should not normally be evident in a baby who has yet to learn to crawl. When children are young and experimenting, it is perfectly normal to find bruises on bony sites. However, damage to soft tissues is less likely to occur accidentally. This includes bruises to the cheeks, thighs, buttocks, and on the back and chest.

In order to obtain the full picture, we need to try and get an explanation for the injury from the child or parent, or both. The question to ask at this stage is whether the explanation given for the injury is plausible or not. Accidental injury to soft tissue sites can happen, but is much less likely than for bony areas. Does the story fit? Is the story the same from parent and child? Is the child telling different people different stories? Asking for explanations for injuries can be difficult. You will need to be tactful and avoid antagonizing the child or parent. You might comment on the injury and ask how it came about, or ask the child if he has any pain and then ask what the causes were. You could tell the parent you are concerned about the injury and then ask how it happened. Sometimes both child and parent will volunteer an explanation. You still need to assess whether this explanation matches the injury or not. For example, in one case, a 5-year-old boy with facial bruising told his teacher that he had fallen off his bike. When his mother arrived to collect him, she told the teacher that he had fallen down on the landing. Both stories could have been plausible on their own, but the teacher was concerned to have two totally different explanations for the same injuries.

Example

Mark, a 7-year-old boy, went to school with bruises on his face which covered part of his forehead and extended round the side of his face. He told his teacher that he had tripped and fallen on his face. She quite rightly felt that there would have been other facial injuries if this had been the case, and also that as the bruises went round the corner of the forehead, that they were inconsistent with a fall on a hard flat surface. The teacher put this information together with her previous concerns about the child who had had other odd bruises, and her feeling that the child was unhappy and under stress. She passed on her concerns which were well justified, in that the investigating social worker found that the injuries had been inflicted by the boy's mother.

Children who appear with injuries that are not properly explained should always have the injuries investigated. However, other explanations than abuse should be sought first. Some children are naturally adventurous, gathering cuts and bruises on a regular basis. Other children may suffer from illnesses or conditions such as brittle-bone disease which make them vulnerable to injury. Physical indicators should always be considered alongside behavioural indicators, in order to look at the whole child. The most common indicators of physical abuse are listed on page 55.

A Chance to Think

One of the problems of child protection is that it is all too easy to focus on the cut or the bruise or the symptom of possible abuse. The child as a person can sometimes be forgotten. So, when we are concerned about possible abuse we should ask ourselves this question: 'Does the explanation given fit the injury or symptom for this child in these circumstances, at the child's current stage of development?'

Concerns should focus on the individual child, and not on some abstract notion of whether certain signs always mean abuse has taken place. The charts of indicators should be used as guidelines only.

 ## Exercise 3

Figure 3.2 shows two outlines each of a baby and a young child. On the left-hand diagrams mark in the sites where you think the baby and child possibly could be accidentally injured. Write down the type of injury that is likely at the site, e.g. bruising. On the right-hand diagrams mark in the sites where you think a baby and a child may receive non-accidental injuries. Write in the type of injury that is likely at the site. Compare your diagrams to those in Appendix II.

Remember that some injuries can be accidental and some non-accidental, so we must look at the physical signs of abuse in the context of the child's whole situation, and the explanation given for the injury. Be careful with explanations, they can be very plausible while still being untrue. One example of this is a toddler who had a black eye. The parents told the childcare workers that the child had run into the living-room doorknob, and this explanation was accepted, until one worker noticed that the child was several inches too short to have received the injury in this way.

BABY (MOBILE)   **BABY (MOBILE)**

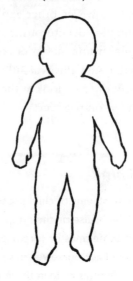

YOUNG CHILD   **YOUNG CHILD**

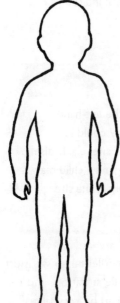

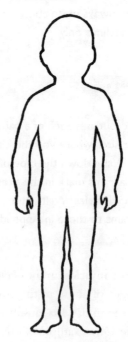

Figure 3.2   Baby and child injuries (accidental and non-accidental)

Recognizing Physical Abuse

1. Fingertip bruising on the body, arms and legs, which may indicate that the child has been gripped hard. Such bruising on the body (front and back) may indicate that the child has been shaken.

2. Bruising that shows the shape of a hand or other object with which the child may have been hit.

3. Bruising to the cheeks, particularly in babies, sometimes accompanied by a torn frenulum, which may indicate that the child has been gripped by the face during force-feeding or attempts to stop him crying.

4. Bruises of different ages, e.g. different colours.

5. Any bruising on a young baby who is not yet mobile.

6. Small round burns, which may be caused by a cigarette. Accidental cigarette burns tend to be less deep and more 'tadpole' shaped. Multiple cigarette burns.

7. Black eyes, particularly where the explanation is inconsistent, e.g. a fall on a flat surface.

8. Burns and scalds in unusual places, or with a neatly defined shape. Accidental burns and scalds are likely to be of an irregular shape. It is sometimes possible to see the shape of the heat source in the burn, e.g. the bar of an electric fire.

9. Bite marks. These may be attributed to another child, but doctors can usually tell the difference between a child's bite and an adult's bite.

10. Internal injuries can result in pain, fever, vomiting, restlessness and difficult breathing.

11. Broken bones may result in the child sitting or standing awkwardly, being unable to move easily, holding a limb in an odd position, and generally seeming to be in pain.

12. Head injuries can result in drowsiness, faintness, fits, vomiting, unconsciousness and coma. The child may appear quiet, pale or purplish, and generally unwell. The child's eyes may roll up. Shaking a young child can cause severe damage to the membranes between the brain and skull resulting in blood clots that can cause brain damage or death.

13. Unlikely or inconsistent explanations for injuries.

14. Untreated injuries.

Children who are physically abused may also show some of the behavioural indicators of emotional stress as outlined below. Living with the fear of not knowing when the next blow might fall or what behaviour might trigger that blow, and the additional strain of lying to other adults and concealing injuries may well result in changed behaviour and signs of emotional distress.

Emotional Abuse

Children who are emotionally abused may show the pain and stress that they are feeling through a range of different behaviours. All children may behave in these ways for other reasons, e.g. bereavement, separation of parents, loss of the family home, long-term illness in the family, a move to a new school or any other event in that child's life that causes stress and unhappiness. So, if a child exhibits some of the behaviours outlined on page 59, it is important to look for obvious explanations first. However, if a child shows patterns of different or difficult behaviour, and there is no obvious reason why, it is worth considering abuse as a possible explanation.

Emotional abuse is often recognized because of the disruptive or difficult behaviour of the child, which may draw attention to the child's needs. Children who are threatened with punishments if they tell anyone about their abuse may bring attention to their plight through negative behaviour, such as attacks on other children, deliberate disobedience and disruptive behaviour. Children are often angry and confused if they have been abused by those they love, feeling a sense of betrayal. They may well take this anger and frustration out in settings away from the home.

Often difficult behaviour contains a message to the childcare worker. It is sometimes hard to understand this message when dealing with a very difficult child, but children do not behave badly without a reason, and that reason may be abuse. So, if faced with a particularly disobedient, disruptive, aggressive child, it is important to take time away from managing that behaviour to ask why the child might be behaving in this way.

It is not likely that a child, even an older child or adolescent, will find it easy to sit down with an adult and describe what is happening in her or his life in clear and rational sentences. It is much more likely that the child will 'act out' their feelings in this way. The important message here is to look for reasons why a child is behaving in difficult and disruptive ways.

Example

Kevin is 6 years old, the middle child of five boys. He was referred to a child psychologist because of his persistent bed-wetting, which his parents had 'tried everything' to stop. At around the same time, the school asked the educational psychologist to see Kevin and his family because of his difficult and demanding behaviour, and his persistent assaults on other children, which had become a major problem within the school.

The clinical psychologist visited Kevin in the boy's own home, and tried to establish a 'star chart' system to reward Kevin for dry nights. However, Kevin's father was unhappy about this approach, arguing that the child should be punished not rewarded. It became clear that Kevin's father could not bring himself to praise Kevin at all, and that his mother took her lead from her husband in terms of her attitude towards Kevin. The parents complained bitterly about every aspect of Kevin's behaviour, comparing him unfavourably to the other children, and singling him out as the 'problem child'. Kevin's behaviour at home was very attention-seeking, and he was often tearful and angry. However, it became clear that the other children were rarely reprimanded for misbehaviour, and Kevin was usually blamed for any naughtiness involving more than one child. The father was punishing Kevin by a series of threats, assaults and ritual humiliations (calling him a 'wimp' and 'a baby').

The psychologist concluded that Kevin was being persistently 'scapegoated' for a number of problems within the family, including marital problems, that had been around for years. The family attended therapy sessions to try and resolve some of these problems, but in the mean time Kevin went to live in a foster home and began to enjoy life. Although Kevin's parents did eventually resolve some of their difficulties, Kevin had become settled in his new home. It was felt that moving Kevin back to his family was too risky and so he stayed with and was later adopted by his foster family. His parents did not contest the adoption order. Kevin was very keen to become legally part of his new family, and made it clear that he did not want to live with his birth family again.

Kevin kept in contact with all his family initially, but contact visits were very difficult for both Kevin and his foster carers. He often displayed aggressive and distressed behaviour after the visits, and was reluctant to go on some occasions. Eventually, the visits were reduced to twice yearly, by mutual consent. Kevin's father rarely attended any of the contact visits. Kevin kept in touch with his mother and siblings by letter, phone and casual contact after his adoption as he continued to live in the same area as his birth family.

A Chance to Think

 Although the profound long-term effects of emotional abuse are well documented, it continues to be difficult to prove that a child has been emotionally abused, especially if there have been no other types of abuse taking place at the same time.

Exercise 4

1. Write down the reasons why you think it is difficult to prove that a child has been emotionally abused, and compare your answers with those in Appendix II.
2. Follow the chart below. For each child write the types of behaviour you would expect in a child of that age in the left-hand column. In the right-hand column write in any behaviours that you would find worrying in a child of that age.

	Expected behaviour	Unusual behaviour
Leah 18 months		
Billy 3 years		
Jane 4 years		
Sam 6 years		
Terry 8 years		
Eve 13 years		

Compare your answers with those in Appendix II.

The most common indicators of emotional abuse are listed below.

Recognizing Emotional Abuse

1. **The child may become withdrawn and isolated, not wanting to mix with peers, and wary of adults.**
2. **Aggressive and/or attention-seeking behaviour, e.g. persistent naughtiness, soiling or wetting on purpose, attacking other children.**
3. **Disturbances of eating and sleeping patterns.**
4. **Tantrums and outbursts that are inappropriate to the child's age and stage of development.**
5. **Regression, where the child wishes to act and be treated like a younger child, e.g. bed-wetting.**
6. **Running away, or hiding.**
7. **Poor performance at school or in nursery activities, loss of confidence and low self-esteem.**
8. **Self-neglect, e.g. wearing the same clothes continuously, refusing to have hair brushed.**
9. **Psychosomatic illnesses.**
10. **Clinging to another adult, wariness and fear of parents.**
11. **Failure to thrive, e.g. poor levels of growth and development, low weight and height, unhealthy appearance.**
12. **Drug and alcohol abuse.**
13. **Truanting.**
14. **Self mutilation.**

Children who have been emotionally abused often suffer other types of abuse also, so these indicators may be apparent alongside the signs of physical or sexual abuse or neglect.

'Failure to thrive' may seem a more appropriate symptom of neglect, but there is a well-documented link between restricted growth and development, and emotional abuse or emotional neglect. Children literally fail to develop properly, if their emotional needs are not met.

Sexual Abuse

There has been a great deal of publicity around all aspects of the sexual abuse of children in recent years, and this may have given the impression that recognizing sexual abuse depends entirely on either the child's disclosure of abuse, or complex medical findings. A child who is suspected of being sexually abused may be examined for medical evidence to provide proof for the courts, but often it is other indicators which draw attention to the abuse in the first place.

Sexual abuse often comes to light through behavioural indicators, including those described for emotional abuse. Children who are sexually abused usually show signs of emotional distress, and can behave in very difficult ways. As with other types of abuse, it is important to remember that children who behave in these ways are trying to let those around them know that there is a problem. Because of the major social taboos surrounding sexual abuse of children, it is vitally important to the abuser that the secret is kept. However, we need to bear in mind that sexual abuse is a reality for many children. It is estimated that up to 1 in 4 girls and 1 in 8 boys may be sexually abused. Many adults deal with the consequences of child sexual abuse throughout their lifetimes, and this may include some of you who are reading this chapter.

Children who are sexually abused are often threatened with terrible consequences, for example, that they will be killed if they disclose the abuse, or separated permanently from their families. At the very least, these children may be told that they will be disbelieved and punished for lying. Sexually abused children find it particularly difficult to voice the enormity of what is happening to them, because they recognize the 'wrongness' and often take the blame upon themselves. However, these children will often strive to get the message across to their carers in a variety of ways. For some of these children, it is easier to pass their message to carers outside the family, particularly if there is a close and trusting relationship with another adult. Many sexual abuse disclosures by children take place at school and nursery.

However, disclosure of sexual abuse does not always take place as a single event. A child may well 'test the water' to see if their chosen adult will be able to cope with what they are being told. Disclosure may be partial, or may involve some untruths or be retracted. For example, one 6-year-old girl who disclosed abuse to her childminder, started the process by telling the childminder that a stranger was coming into her room at night and touching her genitals. She gave quite an elaborate description of the stranger. The childminder doubted very much that this was true, but felt that the child had some reason for the story. She accepted the child's story at face value, which gave the child opportunity to go on to reveal that the 'stranger' was in fact her stepfather. The child was seeking a way forward, while unsure of what would happen when she told the full story. A 15-year-old girl accused her teacher, a stranger and a neighbour, of sexually abusing her before disclosing that she had been abused by her father. Despite being labelled a liar and trouble-maker, the girl persisted with her story, which was later shown to be true. The girl made the earlier accusations because she thought that she would be taken into care and the abuse would stop without her having to tell anyone that her father was the perpetrator. In this way, she felt she could protect her mother and younger sister.

As with other forms of abuse, the apparent behavioural indicators of sexual abuse may have other causes, and these should be explored first. Children under any type of stress may behave differently, or display disruptive or difficult behaviour. The physical signs of possible sexual abuse may have other explanations also. For example, a child may have pain and soreness around the vagina or penis because of a urinary infection.

Example

Alan, a 10-year-old boy, began to be very aggressive in the school playground, hitting and kicking other children, swearing at them and threatening them. Alan also came to school very early, and hung around for a long time after school. When he was told off about his behaviour he became very upset and sometimes hysterical. His school work was poor, and he was disruptive in class. Alan was too thin, and often had bruises on his upper arms, back and chest. Alan would not discuss the bruises with adults, but when asked about them would give an unlikely explanation, often varying the story several times.

Alan also behaved oddly towards his women teachers, making sexual comments about them, and on several occasions deliberately touching their breasts. Finally, Alan was caught in a serious assault on another child. Part of the assault seemed to involve an attempt to push a stick into the other child's anus. During the resulting investigation, Alan, in a highly distressed state, disclosed that he had been sexually and physically abused by his father, being forced to simulate sexual intercourse with his mother, and threatened with the direst punishments if he revealed any of his story to any other adult. Alan was removed to foster parents for his own safety and because he was terrified at the idea of going home. Subsequent investigations found that Alan had been used in compiling pornographic videos and photographs, which his father then sold.

Alan was made the subject of a Care Order, but was eventually rehabilitated to his mother after she had separated from his father.

A Chance to Think

Sexual play is usual in children of different ages and stages of development, as a normal part of exploratory behaviour. Babies and toddlers may masturbate because it gives them nice feelings. Older children may play games that involve looking at or touching each other's genitals. Adolescents will experiment with different sexual behaviours as they mature sexually and emotionally. Children will ask questions about where babies come from and also about adult sexual activities.

It may seem difficult to separate these normal developmental activities from the indicators of sexual abuse. Similarly, parents can often feel threatened that their everyday family behaviour may be misinterpreted as abusive, especially as there is a wide range of beliefs as to what is acceptable. For example, whereas some parents may never appear undressed before their children, others may bath with their children and walk around the house with no clothes on.

 Exercise 5

1. Think of the children you work with. Write down the sorts of questions you might expect them to ask about sexual activity, and the sorts of sexual experimentation or play you might expect from this age group. Ask a colleague what he/she thinks of your list, and whether he/she would add anything to it. Compare your list to the answer in Appendix II.

2. The list of indicators below includes 'sexual knowledge and/or behaviour that seems inappropriate to a child's age and maturity'. Write down what this might mean for the children in your care, and compare your list with the answer in Appendix II.

The list of indicators for child sexual abuse is outlined below.

Recognizing Sexual Abuse

1. Soreness, redness, bruising and cuts around the genitals or anus.

2. Pain or discomfort around the vagina or penis, or the anus.

3. Discomfort or difficulty in walking and sitting.

4. Discharge or bleeding from the vagina or penis.

5. Pain during urination.

6. Sexual knowledge and/or behaviour that seems inappropriate to a child's age and maturity.

7. Sexual play with other children that demonstrates sophisticated knowledge.

8. Running away, anxiety, despair.

9. Fear of certain adults, withdrawal from other children.

10. Acting out sexual scenes through play, or drawing.

11. Regressive behaviour, e.g. thumb-sucking, wetting the bed, fear of the dark.

12. Anger, hostility, aggression towards adults and other children.

13. Behaviour and achievements in nursery or school deteriorate.

14. Sleep and eating disturbances.

15. Telling lies.

16. Unexplained or psychosomatic illnesses.

17. Persistent masturbation.

18. Self-dramatizing behaviour, e.g tantrums, attention-seeking behaviour, elaborate fantasies, hysterical attacks, weeping fits.

19. Disclosure to an adult, possibly a partial or unconvincing account of the abuse, which may then be retracted.

20. Promiscuity, pregnancy, sexually transmitted diseases.

Children who are sexually abused when very young may not know that all families do not behave in this way. They may talk about their abuse quite openly, or portray it through drawings or play. Older children may be more aware that what is happening to them is not acceptable to others, and they may conceal the abuse because they are ashamed or because they fear the consequences of telling. However, sexual abuse raises strong and conflicting feelings in children, and these tend to come out in one way or another.

Example

Seven-year-old twin sisters both began to behave strangely in school, becoming inattentive in class and avoiding other children at break. Instead of concentrating in class or playing with others, they huddled together whispering anxiously. Teachers were puzzled because the children had always seemed happy and well adjusted. Eventually, the children told a teacher that they had been systematically sexually assaulted by a babysitter who was an old and trusted friend of the family. He had threatened to 'kill them with a big stick' if they told their parents. These clever little girls had been slowly working out for themselves that, as the abuser had said not to tell their parents, they might get away with not being 'killed' if they told a different adult. This man had been a trusted friend of the family since before the girls were born, and was seen as an authority figure by them. They had taken his threats very seriously, while realizing that what he was doing was wrong.

Neglect

Neglect of children can be very difficult to clearly determine. In an unequal society children have different levels of care, often determined by levels of income and other resources. It can be difficult to tell the difference between a child who is wilfully neglected, and one whose family simply cannot afford the basics. However, there are a number of indicators that can show that a child may not be getting basic care. Emotional abuse is part of neglect in that emotional needs are as important as physical needs. However, as emotional abuse is dealt with separately, we will concentrate on physical neglect in this section. Children who are neglected are often physically abused also, and usually suffer some level of emotional abuse.

The symptoms of neglect may be apparent among children who have chronic conditions, or who are recovering from illness or injury. Developmental delays can be the result of many different events, such as family traumas – bereavement, divorce, a new baby. Any illness can result in a brief delay in development. Children also develop at different rates, and may have lulls in their development followed by periods of rapid growth, both physically and cognitively. However, any developmental delays should be investigated to find the underlying reason if they persist beyond short-term. Neglect is one of the possible causes that should be considered.

A child who is inappropriately dressed, dirty and smelly may not be the subject of deliberate neglect, but may come from a family where resources are limited. It is difficult to feed children on good, wholesome food on a low income, and it may also be difficult to keep a child clean and fresh when there is no washing machine and hot water cannot be regularly afforded. Cheap clothes soon look tatty, and may not provide enough warmth. Items such as coats and boots may be simply unaffordable. Many families struggle to cope on incomes that do not meet basic needs. The Child Poverty Action Group (CPAG) carried out research which showed that children growing up in families on benefit during the 1980s were notably shorter and less able at school than children from families with higher incomes. Neglect may be apparent, but it may not always be due to poor parenting. Children from ethnic minority families may be over-represented among the worst off in our society, and this may be reflected in standards of care. We have to be careful not to judge the care of children from different social classes and cultures entirely by our own standards.

Some forms of neglect are more clear cut, such as omitting to take a child for medical treatment as necessary, or starving a child, or not giving a child clothing or bedding. One of the best indicators of neglect is the child's height and weight chart although, like any other indicator of abuse, we need to be aware that neglect is only one possible explanation for a child being underweight and/or short of stature.

Example

Tony was a small, underweight 2-year-old, who always appeared to have some ailment – a constantly running nose and a persistent cough and frequent 'tummy upsets'. He looked pale, and in colder weather, purplish and mottled. Tony was usually listless, and his development was slow. In nursery, Tony showed little interest in play or the other children, clinging to the nursery nurse and 'grizzling' for hours at a time. He was hard to stimulate and rarely smiled. Tony would fall asleep over meals and at odd times in the day, and although he seemed hungry he did not like the dinners, only eating sweet things. His speech was very delayed and unclear. He was easily upset, but did not get angry, instead crying weakly for long periods of time. Tony looked grubby, and often wore smelly clothes. He usually arrived at nursery with a dirty nappy, and there was no evidence of any attempts to potty-train him.

The social worker who organized the nursery place reported that Tony's single mother had a totally chaotic lifestyle, with no routine for the children, and no proper meal times. The children ran around with no clothes on at home although the house was cold, and clean clothes were rare. On one occasion the social worker found a basket of clean clothes that had been pushed under the stairs for a month because the cat had had diarrhoea on them. At home Tony drank cola from a baby's bottle, and ate crisps and biscuits. He had no toys, and was rarely spoken to unless to be reprimanded. When Tony went to foster parents because another child in the family had been physically abused by the mother's boyfriend, his weight rose dramatically and his appearance changed within a very short period of time. He lost his pale, dull look and became an active, happy, chatty little boy. He became dry in a few weeks, and lost his persistent cough.

A Chance to Think

We may have very subjective views about neglect. If it is normal in our family to bath and put on clean clothes on a daily basis, we may see a child who only gets bathed once a week as neglected. Similarly, if we believe children should have three wholesome hot meals a day, we may see a child who has mainly cold meals, or convenience food as being neglected.

Some children will describe themselves as ill-treated if they do not own the latest fashion in trainers! More seriously, it is important to note that the majority of neglect cases are among families living on benefits.

Exercise 6

Write down a list of what you think are a child's basic needs, being as specific as you can. Compare your list to the one at the beginning of Appendix II.

The indicators of neglect are outlined below.

Recognizing Neglect

1. Poor levels of physical development, being underweight and short in stature for the child's age.

2. The child may appear thin and look generally unhealthy.

3. The child may be listless, pale and unkempt.

4. Poor hygiene, e.g. dirty, smelly clothes, unwashed body and hair, persistent nappy rash.

5. Lack of interest, difficult to stimulate.

6. Persistent minor illnesses, e.g. colds, coughs, diarrhoea.

7. Illnesses and injuries that have not been attended to, e.g. untreated infections.

8. Inadequate clothing.

9. Hungry, overeating when food is available.

10. Tiredness.

11. The child may be persistently late to school or frequently miss school, although older children may hang around before and after school.

12. Unresponsive to adults or indiscriminate in seeking attention from adults.

13. Sudden and noticeable improvements in all aspects of the child's behaviour and appearance when there is a change in the care situation.

Neglect is often difficult to prove, mainly because the effects of neglect could be due to so many other causes, and because the effects are often slowly accumulating rather than instantly noticeable. Neglect is also a very subjective concept, in that we all have different standards, and what may be perfectly acceptable in one family, may not be in another. For instance, in some families children may run around in the house undressed or just in nappies, whereas in other areas this may not be considered acceptable. Standards of diet vary widely also, for example, some parents are very strict about sweets and crisps, whereas other children have a constant supply. Other children may eat mainly convenience foods, rather than home-cooked foods. Perhaps the main criteria is whether the child seems well and happy or not.

Conclusion

There are no magic ways of knowing if a child has been abused or not, and there are no indicators that will always definitely 'prove' that abuse has taken place. Most of the signs and symptoms outlined above could have explanations other than abuse. This uncertainty can leave the childcare worker feeling unsure of when to act, and unsure whether there is anything to act upon. There can seem to be a yawning gap between jumping to conclusions and over-reacting, and doing nothing while signs and symptoms pile up. However, there are a number of ways in which this uncertainty can be reduced to give the worker confidence to act appropriately. For those of you who work alone, see Chapter 1 for comments on the 'appropriate person' to discuss your concerns with. It is important that you and your colleague or friend pay careful attention to issues of confidentiality when discussing concerns about a child. It could be damaging to the child, the family and to yourself if confidentiality is broken. Be sure you discuss your concerns with someone who is trustworthy and discreet.

1. Always discuss any concerns with your colleagues. They may have information that will help provide a clearer picture, e.g. they may know of other reasons to explain certain signs and symptoms, or they may have concerns of their own about the child.
2. Discuss concerns with the parents, who may have an explanation for the child's condition and behaviour. Check if the explanation fits with the indicators. For example, if a parent tells you that a child has a sore bottom because of a fall on to a bicycle cross-bar, does this fit in with the length of time the child has been sore, and does it fit in with the child's story?

3. It is also useful to gauge the parents' attitude towards the child in general. Are they concerned and interested in the child? Have they sought medical advice as appropriate? Remember that any parent may become flustered and angry if they feel that they are being accused of abusing their child, and this is not necessarily an indication that they are responsible for any harm to the child.

4. Keep records so that any patterns of indicators can emerge, and the whole picture can be seen.

5. Use your knowledge of child development. Is this a 'normal' phase for a child of this age and stage of development to be going through? For example, a child of 2, who has just been presented with a baby sister or brother may well want to behave like a baby themselves, or be naughty and disruptive, or be aggressive towards the baby, or start bed-wetting again and waking in the night. This would all be part of the child's normal reaction to the 'competition'. These indicators might be viewed differently if they appeared for no apparent reason.

6. Listen to what the child has to say to you. Sometimes worries and concerns can be clarified simply by spending a little time with the child.

Finally, remember the limits of your role, and do not feel that you have to be absolutely certain that abuse is taking place before you discuss your concerns with the appropriate person. Trust your instincts and your knowledge of the children in your care and, when in doubt, remember that it is better to act and be wrong, than not to act at all.

Further Reading

Child Protection Procedures (available from local library).

Cloke, C. and Naish, J. (1992) *Key Issues in Child Protection*, Harlow, Longman.

Croll, L. (1991) *Caring for Children and Young People Who Have Been Sexually Abused*, Winnipeg, Naturas Inc.

Erooga, M. and Masson, H. (1990) *Investigations – Journeys into the Unknown (a Guide to Investigating Physical Abuse and Neglect)*, Rochdale, Rochdale Child Protection Training Sub-Committee.

O'Hagan, K. (1993) *Emotional and Psychological Abuse of Children*, Buckingham, The Open University Press.

Stainton Rogers, W., Hevey, D. and Ash, E. (1989) *Child Abuse and Neglect – Facing the Challenge*, London, B.T. Batsford Ltd.

4

Responding to Suspected Abuse

Introduction

In the last chapter, we discussed how you might recognize possible signs and symptoms of child abuse. Perhaps the next question you may be asking is: 'If I am fairly sure that there is reason to believe that abuse has taken place, what do I do next?' To some extent, the answer to this question may seem fairly simple, i.e. pass the problem on to somebody else! However, the way in which you initially deal with your suspicions and the skills that you demonstrate in dealing with the child and family at this stage can be crucial in ensuring the success of any child protection measures that are then taken.

Although other professionals will be investigating the suspected abuse, it is very likely that you will remain in the 'frontline' working with the child and her family. It is also possible that you are one of the people outside the family who have the most contact with the child – which is probably why you came to suspect abuse in the first place.

In this chapter we will look at your responsibilities as a childcare worker for reporting suspected child abuse, some of the issues around reporting and how you can use your interpersonal skills to their best advantage in what can be a very difficult and emotionally charged situation.

There are a number of ways in which child abuse may come to your notice and we shall explore these in turn. The way in which you come to suspect abuse may affect how you respond to it. You may notice signs and symptoms of abuse as outlined in Chapter 3, or someone else may report their suspicions to you, e.g. another parent or worker. Or the child may tell you about abuse either directly or indirectly. This is called 'disclosure'. It may be that abuse comes to your notice by a combination of means, i.e. you may have your own growing concerns about a child confirmed by another person. It is not a clear-cut procedure and there may be a series of events before you feel that the time has come to act on your suspicions.

It is vitally important to keep a record of growing concerns, so that information passed to others at a later date will be accurate and truthful. The different ways in which suspicions of abuse can be generated will be explored in detail below, including ideas about how you might respond in different circumstances. We will then look at how to report suspected child abuse and to whom you should report your concerns.

Disclosure of Abuse by the Child

Disclosure of child abuse is usually from children who have the verbal skills to tell someone about what is happening to them. As such, there are many children who will not be able to disclose their abuse. These will include pre-verbal children and children with physical and verbal disabilities which impair their communication. One of the reasons that these groups of children may be particularly vulnerable to child abuse is because they cannot speak out.

Infants under 1 year old are statistically more likely to be abused than older children and there is a growing awareness among professionals in child protection that abuse of disabled children may be much more prevalent than is generally thought. Children from black and Asian families who have experienced racism may find it difficult to trust a white childcare worker enough to venture a disclosure of abuse. Childcare workers need to be aware that some groups of children can only express their pain and sadness in non-verbal ways, not through disclosure.

Children who disclose abuse often do so with a considerable amount of forethought, sometimes with one or more trial runs or false starts, and often after a long period of preparing for the response they might get. If a child chooses you to disclose to, this often implies that you are a person that they trust a great deal. Disclosing abuse is often extremely difficult for a child, especially if the child has been threatened with punishment if they divulge the abuse. Most children only have the vaguest of ideas about what might happen if abuse is disclosed and they may be fearful of the consequences of telling what they know. A child may test out the adult they wish to disclose to, by asking 'what if?' questions, or raising the issue of abuse in a roundabout manner.

For example, one teenage girl disclosed that she had been assaulted by a schoolteacher, and then retracted the accusation, to immediately replace it with accusations against a male neighbour, an older boy and a mysterious stranger. Although those around her

Good Practice Issues

- Listen to the children in your care, as a child may well disclose in a crowded room, at the toilet, at lunch or at play, because children do not have an adult sense of the 'right' place and time.
- If a child says something important at a time when it is impossible to stop and listen, acknowledge this and tell the child that you will talk to them later.
- Let the child talk to you in their own way and in their own time without jumping to conclusions or interrupting.
- Be open and honest with the children you care for so they can develop trust in you.
- If you care for a number of children, make time to give each child individual attention on a regular basis, even if only for a few minutes.
- Be approachable and available.
- Trust your 'third ear' which is the instinct, based on knowledge and experience, which tells you when something is amiss.
- Avoid stereotypes and assumptions about what are 'normal' childrearing practices in families from different racial and cultural backgrounds from your own.

despaired of her lying, it was clear to the professionals involved that something was severely wrong in this child's life. Eventually, the child disclosed that she had been raped by her father on a number of occasions which he later confirmed to be true. The child's earlier accusations had been a combination of 'cry for help' and testing out the response she might get to a disclosure. Fortunately, despite the distress that her false accusations caused, this child was dealt with very sensitively and not dismissed as a malicious liar, so that she was eventually able to trust an adult enough to disclose her secret.

It is also possible that if a child is not regularly abused, or has not been threatened with punishment if they tell, that he may quite simply disclose to an adult, perhaps in response to a casual question about a bruise or injury. However, many disclosures do not take place as a single event and may arrive in a disjointed, piecemeal fashion over a period of time. The child's confusion may be expressed through other means prior to a disclosure, including behavioural symptoms, drawings and paintings and play activities which reflect the child's state of mind.

There are a number of good practice issues that we should consider in order to maximize the chances of a child being able to successfully disclose to you, which are outlined in the box opposite. These are not just about good practice with children who are suspected of being abused, but are relevant to all our work with children. Consider them as methods of 'keeping the door open' for any child who wishes to disclose abuse.

The aim of good practice is to ensure that we avoid blocking a possible disclosure through lack of time, dismissing the child's story, being unapproachable, or making assumptions about what the child is telling us. Before good procedures were developed, many children disclosed abuse to find their stories dismissed or ignored, or simply not responded to. This is particularly true in the case of sexual abuse. Many of today's adults who were sexually abused in childhood report that they tried at the time to disclose the abuse was taking place but with no success. A child who is not believed or responded to when they disclose abuse may well not try and disclose a second time. A child who sees disclosure as a way out of an intolerable situation may despair if their only hope is dashed and the feeling of being trapped in a nightmare situation may well cause profound and long-term emotional damage.

A Chance to Think

It is sometimes useful to rehearse in your own mind how you might respond in difficult situations, so that you are not completely taken by surprise if such a situation occurs. Remember that your initial response is crucially important in the child protection process and so it should always be a considered rather than a spontaneous response. The child may well retract or discontinue the disclosure if your response is seen as unhelpful.

 Exercise 1

Imagine that a child in your care starts to tell you things that are happening to him and you realize that he is disclosing abuse:

1. What do you think you would feel at that point in time?
2. How would you respond to the child?

Compare your answers with the sample answers in Appendix II.

Perhaps the key to 'keeping the door open' for children to talk to us is the ability to listen. It is easy to regard communication as being about talking, but the most important skill is in allowing and encouraging others to talk to us. Many counselling skills are techniques to encourage others to talk to us, and it may be useful for you to read more about these if you are unsure about your own listening skills.

Complete the ticklist in Exercise 2 to get an idea of the strengths and weaknesses of your own listening skills.

Exercise 2: Listening Skills

	Rarely	Sometimes	Often
1. How often do you interrupt others while they are talking?			
2. Do you finish sentences for other people?			
3. Do you show that you are listening, e.g. by eye contact?			
4. Do you assume you know what others are going to tell you?			
5. Are you too busy to listen?			
6. Do you give advice as soon as someone starts to tell you a problem?			
7. Do you make opportunities for others to talk to you?			

Compare your answers to those in Appendix II. You may wish to take some time over this exercise, by monitoring over a few days how you listen to others, and in this way become more aware of your own strengths and weaknesses.

Procedures and Guidelines for Responding to Abuse

It may be helpful for you to discuss procedures for dealing with disclosure with the appropriate person before it happens to you, so that you know that you are following agency guidelines where available. Always ask if there are written guidelines as to what is expected of you in this situation and, if there is nothing in writing, ask the appropriate person what they would expect you to do.

Each area has local guidelines for agencies and workers involved in childcare, which outline the roles and responsibilities of the various parties when child abuse is suspected or known. These are called Child Protection Procedures and are usually produced locally by the Area Child Protection Committee (ACPC), a group of senior representatives from all the local agencies involved in child protection, e.g. police, education, probation, health and, of course, social services. The Child Protection Procedures also provide a framework for action in response to suspected child abuse, to ensure that the response is thorough and consistent. They also have a major role in ensuring that the various workers and agencies involved in child protection work closely and co-operatively together, as detailed in the government document *Working Together under the Children Act, 1989 – a Guide to Inter-Agency Co-operation for the Protection of Children from Abuse* issued by the Department of Health in 1991. Social services will have copies of the procedures, and you should have access to a copy if you work in any local authority childcare setting. There may also be copies in your library. These guidelines are soon to be replaced by *Working Together to Safeguard Children* (1998), which was circulated in draft form for consultation in September 1998.

Responding to Disclosure

If a child does disclose abuse to you, your immediate response is very important in both helping the child through what might be a painful and upsetting story and in gathering information that will assist a possible subsequent investigation. The checklist overleaf details some of the factors you might need to bear in mind when making your response to the child.

Responding to Disclosure: Checklist

- Listen to the child and let her tell her story in her own time and way.
- Try not to interrupt or ask questions at this stage, but show you are listening through positive body language.
- Control your feelings of anger or disgust – these are perfectly natural, but the child will not be helped by seeing them and may believe that you are angry or disgusted with them.
- Try not to panic – this is a big responsibility, but you already have the child's trust, which is the most important part.
- Do not promise not to tell anyone else.
- Do reassure the child that she has done the right thing in telling you and that you will take steps to help her although this will involve telling other people what has happened.

If the child is in immediate danger of further abuse, then reporting must be done swiftly as it may be necessary to take steps without delay to protect the child. It may be that you are in the middle of a working day, in which case you should verbally report what the child has told you to the appropriate person as soon as possible, so that they can take action. This will involve calling social services and reporting the situation to the duty social worker. If you work alone then you should call the duty social worker yourself and explain the situation straightaway. Although you will probably make a verbal report initially, it is very important to make a detailed note of what the child has told you as soon as possible, while the information is fresh in your memory. The details of what you should report are outlined later in this chapter.

If the child has disclosed to you outside office hours, you may need to report the abuse to the out-of-hours social work team (sometimes known as the night duty team or the emergency duty team). If you do not know how to contact them then you should find this out now. The phone number should be listed in the local Child Protection Procedures, or should be available from social services, or from the police. If you have any concerns that the child may be in immediate danger of further abuse after leaving your care, then contact the out-of-hours team as soon as you can. Do not take any risks. If an adult who may be involved in the abuse arrives to collect the child before you have reported the abuse, or while you are waiting for a response to your call, do not try and detain the child or discuss the disclosure with that adult. Instead, ring the duty social worker immediately to explain what has happened so that they can act swiftly to protect the child. If the child is too scared to go home then you should explain this in your report so that social services can advise you on how to deal with this eventuality.

It may be that the child is not at immediate risk of further abuse because the abuser is not one of the child's caretakers. In this case, you should still contact social services if the disclosure takes place during office hours, and ask their advice on how to proceed. If the disclosure takes place out of office hours, use your judgement as to whether you need to phone the out-of-hours team or to leave reporting till the following day. In these circumstances, it may be appropriate to tell the adult who collects the child what has happened, unless there is some reason not to do so, e.g. you suspect that adult already knows about the abuse and has not acted to prevent it or you suspect that adult may put pressure on the child to retract her story or you feel that adult may become aggressive or violent towards you or another person. *If in any doubt always contact the duty social worker or out-of-hours team for advice.* They will help you to judge the best course of action and provide you with support.

Try and be discreet in your dealings with the child if there are other people around – they do not all have to know what is happening. Discourage others from asking the child to repeat her story, as she will be asked to do this when the social worker arrives. If the child is distressed, try and stay with her somewhere quiet, away from other children, and if necessary explain as briefly as possible to thers that she does not feel too well. However, remember that you will need support in this situation and if possible you should ask for this from a colleague who will remain calm, act to support you and maintain confidentiality.

Finally, do not let the child become forgotten during the reporting process. Disclosure of abuse can be a highly traumatic experience for the child, and she will need continuing support and encouragement as the process unfolds. You should not underestimate your own role in this – remember that the child disclosed to you because she trusts you and it may be you whom she needs to support her during the early stages of an investigation.

A Chance to Think

 A child who has been abused will have many different feelings to deal with and disclosure may bring some of these feelings out into the open. Every child is a unique individual and so no single child will display a standard set of feelings and responses to being abused. However, many children display anger and fear, feelings of being worthless and unlovable, and feelings of being somehow to blame for the abuse. Children may also show strong feelings towards the abuser and, although these feelings may include dislike or hate, they may also include love for the abuser and concern that the abuser should not suffer through the disclosure. The child may also be angry with other adults for failing to protect her from abuse and may even be angry with you for not detecting the abuse earlier.

Exercise 3

Look back at the case studies of children experiencing different types of abuse in Chapter 2 and write down how you think each of those children might be feeling. Compare your thoughts with the sample answers in Appendix II.

Responding to Suspicions of Abuse

You may come to suspect that a child is being abused because you or another person notices some of the signs and symptoms outlined in the previous chapter. The signs of physical abuse are generally the most easy to interpret, but this should not deter you from reporting other concerns about a child. Unless you are faced with a distinctive injury that fairly clearly could not have occurred accidentally, you will probably gather information about the child over a period of time. If you are in doubt as to whether the information you have is enough to act upon, it is important to talk over your concerns with another knowledgeable person who will maintain confidentiality and support you in the decision you make.

Example

A volunteer at a playgroup for 2–5-year-olds noticed that one of her 3-year-old charges had severe bruising on her face. She remembered that the child had had similar bruising a few months before, for which no explanation had been offered by the mother. The worker also had general concerns about the child, who was very quiet and whose development was noticeably delayed, especially her speech. The worker felt that there was definite cause for concern, but was hesitant as to how to act. She was specifically concerned that they lived in a small community, where everyone knew everyone else. The worker consulted with a friend who also volunteered at the playgroup and who shared the worker's concerns about the child. In the end the worker called the NSPCC and an investigation into the child's situation took place. Although the child was temporarily removed to foster care she was eventually successfully rehabilitated and the family received some much needed help to care better for their children.

If you are concerned about a child who has the necessary verbal skills, it is important to make time to talk to that child and to try and explore what is happening in his life at the time. However, it is very important that you do this in a non-directive manner, so that you do not impose your own assumptions or interpretations on the child's story. A 'non-directive manner' simply means that you listen to the child without interpreting what she is saying or drawing conclusions about her comments or asking leading questions that might put words in the child's mouth. Although you may have your own ideas about what has happened to the child (and you may be right in the conclusions you have drawn) it is important that the child tells her own story. Concerns should also be shared with parents in the same way. Many of your concerns about a child may stem from causes other than abuse, as outlined in the previous chapter. Parents may well wish to share their own concerns and worries with you and might welcome the opportunity to talk if you approach them in a non-accusatory way.

A Chance to Think

 Current childcare legislation emphasizes the need to work in partnership with parents around issues of child protection. Parents can easily feel under attack if the workers who care for their children appear to be accusing them of abusing their child. If you have concerns about a child it may well be that they can be resolved by sharing them with the child's parents. However, this can be a delicate exercise requiring tact and a sympathetic approach.

Exercise 4

You have a 3-year-old child in your care, who has recently shown a number of behavioural changes which have caused you concern. The child has regressed in his behaviour and is starting to wet his pants again, to use baby language, to ask for a bottle, and to lie in the corner of the room in a foetal position hugging a 'suckie' and sucking his thumb. He cries easily, and seems often to be upset for no particular reason. This is not like the child you started to care for six months ago! You decide to approach the child's mother when she collects him and share your concerns with her.

1. Write a list of 'dos' and 'do nots' about how you might approach the child's mother, e.g. do not make accusations, do be calm and friendly. Compare your list with the one opposite.
2. Write down some of the things you might say to the mother in order to start the conversation about your concerns. Compare these with the sample in Appendix II.

If you are approached by another person who expresses concerns about a child, for example someone you work with or another parent, it is important to listen carefully to their concerns and the reasons behind them. You may know some of the reasons for changes in the child's behaviour or appearance and be able to supply these. On the other hand, you may share some of the concerns held by the other person and the conversation may help you to decide to act on these concerns. It is vital that you are absolutely clear which information comes from you firsthand and which is hearsay. Many a child protection investigation has been 'muddied' through confusing what information is known firsthand by an adult involved and what he or she has heard from other sources.

Talking to the Parent about your Concerns

Do:
- voice your concerns in a quiet and undramatic manner
- try and engage the parent in a discussion about the issues
- listen to what the parent has to say
- try and establish a mutual approach to the problems
- recognize that the parent may feel under attack
- talk privately
- respond calmly to any anger or upset.

Do not:
- accuse, or imply that the parent has abused the child
- assume you know more about the child than the parent does
- be angry or judgemental in your approach
- jump to conclusions
- demand explanations
- threaten further action
- breach confidentiality.

Investigating Suspected Abuse

Once abuse has been reported an investigation will take place. If the abuse is considered to be serious from the initial report and/or the child needs immediate medical attention or protection, it is very likely that the investigation will begin the same day. If the child needs immediate medical attention, this must be sought as a priority and the investigation started afterwards. The investigation will usually be carried out by a qualified social worker with training and experience in child protection. However, certain serious types of abuse may also be jointly investigated by a police officer with similar training and experience.

One of the first things that the investigators will do is talk to the person who made the original report. If this is you it is extremely important that you provide the maximum amount of information possible without adding any 'frills', i.e. assumptions, opinions, gossip or embellishments. If information you possess came from another person it is important that you make this clear at the time of passing it on. Use the checklist below to help you make sure that you have included all the relevant information in your report and that the information is presented clearly and coherently. It may be useful to write down your information beforehand in order to present it in a clear and coherent manner. However, do remember that the person taking your report will have the skills and experience to ask you the right questions and to make sense of the information that you give them, so that you do not need to worry unduly about perfect presentation.

Reporting Abuse: Information Checklist

Name of the child

Age of the child and date of birth

Name, address and phone number of the parent(s)/guardian(s) with whom the child lives

Name, address and phone number of any other important adult, e.g. other parent, grandparents

Details of your causes for concern including:
- dates, times and places of incidents
- any indicators of possible abuse (see Chapter 3)
- details of anything the child has said to you
- details of anything the parent(s) have said to you
- allegations by another person
- anyone you have discussed the situation with
- any other person who may have additional information
- if you have reported similar concerns previously
- any other relevant information

Assume that the person you are going to tell has no information about the child or her family at all and do not worry that you are giving too much information – the investigator will have the skills needed to sift out what is relevant or not.

A Chance to Think

You may be thinking by now that it all seems simple in theory, but that the decision to report suspected abuse is much more difficult in practice. There are many reasons why we might decide not to report suspicions of abuse. For example, we might feel that we know the person accused of child abuse well and that we simply cannot believe that they would do such a thing. We might be worried that the child will be removed from home or that the abuser will be aggressive towards us or that it is not any of our business. We might also be concerned about being seen as racist if the child and family are from a different cultural and racial background from our own.

There are any number of reasons not to report suspicions of abuse. But, if abuse is not reported then the child may continue to live in pain and fear, to suffer injuries or, even, to be killed. Many children who have been abused have found their 'cries for help' ignored and many adults have taken the responsibility of ignoring the signs and symptoms of abuse. As a childcare worker you have a professional responsibility to pass suspicions on to the appropriate person, however difficult this might be to do and however concerned you might be about the outcomes. Almost every child death inquiry includes statements from those who suspected that the child was being abused – and who did not act to prevent tragedy.

Exercise 5

1. Draw up a list of reasons why you may not want to report suspicions of child abuse.
2. Write another list of reasons why you think it is always important to report suspicions of abuse.

Compare both lists to those in Appendix II.

After the initial report has been made the investigator will probably interview the child, family members and any other person who might have information relevant to the case. This could include any adult who cares for the child, e.g. nursery staff or childminder, or who is involved with the child professionally, e.g. health visitor or general practitioner (GP), and will also include parents and any other relevant persons.

The child may be interviewed while still in your care and you may be asked to stay and give the child support during the interview. The child may need reassurance and comfort. The interview is kept as short as possible to avoid distress to the child. A social worker usually conducts the interview, but when serious allegations have been made, the interview may be done jointly by the social worker and a trained police officer. Both will probably have had training in sympathetic interview skills and working with children. After the initial interviews a decision will be made as to whether the child should be removed from, or not returned, home on an emergency basis. This decision may require legal action (see Chapter 6).

The Case Conference

During the investigation, a case conference may be convened to pool information about the child and to make recommendations about how the child could be protected in the future. The case conference is multidisciplinary and will include a range of professionals involved with the child, such as the health visitor, GP, paediatrician, police representative, teacher, nursery staff or childminder, the social worker who has been allocated to the case and a case conference chairperson who is often a senior social services officer. It is now usual to involve the child's parents in all or part of a case conference.

The purpose of the case conference is to agree a Child Protection Plan and to organize arrangements for monitoring and reviewing the child's welfare. In order to achieve these aims the case conference members have to ensure that all relevant information is being taken into account when making decisions about the child's future. Imagine a jigsaw puzzle. Each person involved with the child has some pieces of that puzzle, but until they meet and put together those pieces the whole picture is not clear. If recommendations are made on partial information this could lead to unnecessary risks to the child, or to wrong decisions being made about the child's future care. In addition to personnel who attend to pool information about the child and his family circumstances, some people will be at the case conference because they might be able to offer services to help the child and family with any problems that are identified.

It is usual for parents and other relevant family members to be invited to all or part of the case conference. One of the reasons for this is that plans for the child usually need the co-operation and agreement of parents in order to work. Most parents in this situation need support and help and this can best be achieved by planning with them, not for them. Parents who retain some control of the process may feel better about working with the professionals involved in the care plan. *Working Together under the Children Act 1989* (DoH, 1991) recommends developing a partnership with parents to protect children. It can feel uncomfortable to be honest about your concerns when parents are in the same room listening to what you have to say; however, this should not deter you from giving your information clearly and fully. It may help to think about how you can put across your points in a factual way that avoids unnecessary negative comments about the parents.

A Chance to Think

 When we report information to others, the way in which this information is phrased or couched can influence the other person's perception of what is being reported. For example, we could say that a child has been 'battered black and blue' or we could say that the child has 'received extensive bruising to the buttocks and thighs'. It is not easy to avoid dramatic or emotive language when dealing with child abuse, but it may not be helpful when trying to work out an effective care plan which involves parents.

Exercise 6

John is 2 years old and has Down syndrome. You are one of his carers in the nursery he attends to give respite to his parents. A few weeks ago you found bruising on John's buttocks and thighs when you were changing his nappy. You reported your concerns to your manager, including your observations about the rough handling John received from his mother when delivering and collecting him from nursery and her generally angry and negative attitude towards the child. You have also been concerned about the general state of John's health. He seems thin and weak, he cries easily and looks pale and sad. His clothes are not always suitable or clean and he has an air of neglect. John is very clingy with you and you have grown fond of him. You feel angry about the state he is in and the feeling you have that John receives little love and attention when he is not with you. You also passed on your belief that John's father had left the family home which includes two older children.

1. Write down what you would say to make the initial report.
2. Look at what you have written. Think about making your report to a case conference which includes John's parents. Do you need to re-think how you have reported your concerns? What changes would you make and why? Compare your report to the sample report in Appendix II.

It may be that your initial report echoed your feelings of anger about the treatment which you perceived John to be receiving from his parents. Although your feelings might be very natural, they are based on only partial information about John's circumstances. In addition, expressing angry feelings in this situation might not be the best way of helping the child. You may need to discuss your feelings with a trusted colleague or supervisor in order to get help in dealing with them.

The case conference can only recommend, not decide, a care plan for the child because representatives such as social workers, who have legal responsibilities in child protection cases need to be free to act as needed. However, case conference recommendations are generally implemented by the agencies involved and if this is not possible, the reasons why should be passed to the case conference membership. Child protection case conferences do make two decisions, one of which is to allocate a key worker who has the responsibility of co-ordinating work with the child. The key worker is normally a social worker. The case conference also decides whether to place the child's name on the Child Protection Register (sometimes still called the 'at risk' register). This register lists children's names under different categories of abuse and is used by social workers and medical staff primarily, to check whether the child has been subjected to abuse on previous occasions.

The register is also used to indicate to those involved the severity of the concerns about the child and to identify the need for ongoing work with the child and family. In theory, all registered children should have an allocated social worker and regular review case conferences to monitor and evaluate the child's progress and the level of risk to the child. The register is often kept by the social services, but in some authorities may be kept by the NSPCC or a hospital.

Removal of the child's name from the register is also decided by the case conference and indicates that the risk to the child is now considered to be minimal. It may also indicate a reduction in help offered to the child and family from social services and other agencies.

Perhaps you will be invited to attend a case conference about a child who is in your care, even if it was not you who raised concerns about the child. You will be invited because you have valuable information to contribute about the child's health, welfare, state of mind and relationships. You may be able to contribute to information about changes in the child's behaviour and/or appearance, and the child's growth and development. Case conferences can seem very daunting, as they are usually formal meetings. However, your attendance could be vital in ensuring that a full picture of the child, his circumstances and his needs emerges from the meeting.

In order to prepare for your role in a case conference look at the list below, and remember that the chairperson is there to ensure that everyone is enabled to contribute, and that all contributions are taken into account when making recommendations.

Preparing for a Case Conference

It is always useful to write notes about the things you have to say about the child, so that you can present your information clearly and briefly. Case conferences often involve a number of people and it is important that information is presented concisely so that there is time for everyone to have a say. If the chairperson thinks it will be useful for you to discuss any part of your information further, they will ask you to elaborate. The list below contains some of the information that it may be helpful to include in your contribution to a case conference. However, there may be other things you feel it is important to add, because each child's circumstances are unique.

Preparing for a Case Conference: Checklist

1. Describe the nature of your involvement with the child, e.g. as the child's minder, or caring for the child at nursery.
2. Describe how long you have known the child and how frequently you have contact with the child.
3. Detail any specific work or role you have undertaken with the child, e.g. monitoring the child's physical health.
4. Give any details you can about past or present causes for concern about the child, including dates and details of any incidents, and a record of your concerns.
5. Offer relevant information about the child and family circumstances, including information and/or concerns you might have about any other child in the family.
6. Detail any changes you have noted in the child's behaviour or appearance.
7. Give any additional information that may help the case conference make appropriate recommendations.
8. Make it clear when you are speaking from your own knowledge or observations, and when you are passing information from a third party.

Remember that your information may be vital in reaching an understanding of the child's life and circumstances, so even though you may find it difficult to speak in meetings, try to contribute. Perhaps the information that you have contradicts the information given by another person at the meeting. If this happens, it is still important for you to give your version if you believe it to be true, so that any discrepancies can be identified and investigated.

Roles and Responsibilities of the Different Professionals Involved in Child Protection

Social Workers

Social workers are often seen to have primary or sole responsibility for the protection of children, a role that has often exposed them to criticism in the media. In fact, although social workers have a central role in child protection work, other professionals are almost always involved in the assessment and investigation of suspected abuse, and in the decision-making process about the child's life and future. Social workers' activities are also defined and controlled by legal requirements and by the local authority procedures on child protection.

These procedures usually identify a series of steps that the social services will take during an investigation, and which will also involve other professionals, including possibly yourself. These steps include:

- receiving the initial referral and taking basic information from the referrer (see 'Reporting Abuse: Information Checklist' on page 82)
- checking to see if the child's name is on the Child Protection Register
- in cases where the child is in immediate danger of further abuse, taking steps to protect the child on an emergency basis
- allocating the case to a specific worker
- gathering information from a range of individuals involved with the child
- convening a case conference to discuss the risks to the child and to explore alternative plans to protect the child in the future. The case conference will also make decisions about whether to register the child on the Child Protection Register
- implementing the Child Protection Plan which may include taking legal action in respect of the child.

The allocated social worker will always work in consultation with a senior member of staff, and in many social services departments, with advice from specialist child protection officers. The social worker will consult with other professionals involved with the child, for example, health visitors, GPs, teachers, nursery staff or childminders, and any family members or other adults who have a significant relationship with the child. Although current childcare legislation emphasizes working in partnership with parents, this can be difficult if a family member is seen as responsible for the abuse. However, social workers have a legal duty to investigate suspected child abuse cases, and this duty has to be fulfilled, however difficult the circumstances.

Police

The police have a general duty to investigate crime and to gather evidence in order to ensure that suspected criminals are prosecuted. As the abuse of children sometimes involves a crime, the police can be involved in the investigative process. However, in recent years there have been many initiatives to help social workers and police officers to work closely together to ensure that their investigations dovetail, thereby reducing stress to the child and family.

These initiatives involve joint guidelines in most local authorities for working on child protection investigations, and often joint training of social workers and police officers to try and develop a better working relationship between them. The primary aim of the social services is to protect children, while the primary aim of the police is to investigate crime, and there have been many improvements in the working relationship between the two agencies. The police often do not pursue prosecution if it is clearly not in the best interests of the child. Many authorities have joint investigative procedures, where the investigation of serious child abuse is carried out jointly between social workers and police officers, who may interview the child and family together in order to avoid repetition.

Health Visitors and Other Medical Staff

Health visitors have a particular role in monitoring the development of young children under school age, and this places them in a central role in determining any concerns about a child's welfare. Health visitors are often in a unique position to detect signs and symptoms of abuse in pre-school age children. Their detailed records of growth and development can be crucial information in the investigation of possible abuse. Health visitors may therefore play a key role in the investigation of suspected abuse, and in the monitoring of children who are considered to be at risk.

It is normal practice for children who are suspected of having been abused to be medically examined, either by their GP or, more commonly, by a paediatrician at the local accident and emergency unit. The evidence gathered in this way is often used to determine if abuse has taken place, along with other information gathered about the child and family, and may also be used as evidence in any legal proceedings which result from the investigation. However, abuse sometimes comes to light when children are taken to hospital with injuries, or for other reasons, and so other medical staff may be involved in ascertaining suspicions of abuse.

Nursery Staff, Childminders and Teachers

Along with health visitors, nursery staff and childminders have a central role in the care of young children, and may be in a unique position to notice the signs and symptoms of abuse among those children. Workers who have frequent direct contact with children who have been abused, or are suspected of being abused, will also have a monitoring role which may be part of the child's care plan. Teachers have a similar role with older children, resulting in a high percentage of child protection referrals being received from schools. In many local authorities schools have a designated child protection liaison teacher who has a specific role in co-ordinating the school's response to child protection issues. This usually involves working with representatives of the social services and other relevant agencies.

National Society for the Prevention of Cruelty to Children

The NSPCC has a remit to investigate and respond to suspected child abuse cases. Like social services departments, the NSPCC has a legal power to instigate care proceedings with respect to a child who is judged to have been abused. In the current climate of close liaison and 'working together' NSPCC branches work in close co-ordination with their local social services department.

Other Voluntary Organizations

There are a number of other national and local organizations who offer help and support to abused children and adults and their families, such as Childline, and The Family Welfare Association. These organizations are often staffed by trained volunteers as well as paid staff, and have a responsibility to bring to the notice of the social services any concerns they may have about specific children.

Possible Outcomes of the Investigation

One of the questions everyone asks themselves when reporting suspected abuse of a child they know is, 'What will happen to the child?' One of the reasons you may have given for not reporting suspicions of abuse is the fear that this action will lead to the child's removal from home. In fact, only a small number of investigations result in a child being removed from home on even a temporary basis. However, it is useful to be aware of the possible outcomes of a child protection investigation. There are no cast-iron rules which will tell us before the investigation what will happen to a particular child. Each case is unique and the outcome will depend on a large number of complex and interrelated factors.

However, there are a number of outcomes which are possible in a case of suspected abuse. Chapter 5 deals with the different court orders that a child may be subject to, so they will only be touched on briefly here.

First, the investigation may decide that abuse has not taken place and, so, no further action will be taken. In many cases where abuse has taken place, but the child is not considered to be still at risk, the intervention may end with the investigation. This may be because the abuser is not part of the household, or because the abuse is minor and also a one-off. The child may be monitored in her own home by social services and other agencies, while work goes on to improve the care of the child. This may be an informal arrangement or by court order. The person responsible for the abuse may leave the household allowing the child to remain safely there. On the other hand the child may leave the household and go into the care of another person, either on an informal basis or by court order. This may be a temporary or permanent arrangement, depending on whether the risk to the child can be reduced enough to allow her to return home safely.

No decisions about a child's life and future are taken lightly, and before steps are taken to remove a child from the care of its parents on a permanent basis there will be a great deal of discussion and planning, and usually work with the parents to try to make the home a safer place for the child. The decision to try and remove a child from the care of its parents is not made by any one person – it will be a court of law which makes the final decision.

None of these possibilities is mutually exclusive, in that more than one of these strategies may apply to the same child at different times.

Claims of Abuse against Childcare Workers

Some of the more difficult and hard to resolve claims of child abuse are those which are made against childcare workers, who are accused of abuse in their professional capacity. There is evidence that those entrusted with the care of children will in some cases abuse that trust. Efforts have been made in recent years to try and prevent people who already have child abuse convictions from being able to get jobs which bring them into contact with children. This is mainly achieved through a system whereby employers can check an individual's police record before that person is allowed to take up a job with children.

Obviously, this must be done with the person's permission. Despite these precautions, a number of cases arise every year in which carers are found to have abused their charges.

Children who have already suffered abuse may be particularly vulnerable to further abuse, especially in the case of children who have been sexually abused. These days it is usual for a referral of suspected child abuse, where a childcare worker is accused of the abuse, to be dealt with in the same way as any other such case. However, childcare workers can be vulnerable to false accusations and so these situations must be handled sensitively.

A Chance to Think

 In the light of media reporting about accusations of child abuse against childcare workers you may have concerns about this happening to you or one of your colleagues. It can be difficult for any worker to be involved when a colleague becomes subject to a child protection investigation.

Exercise 7

Amy is four. She is a mixed-race child who has a white mother and Asian father. She attends the nursery which you work at three days a week. Amy has been living with white foster carers, Mr and Mrs Smith, for six months now. She was made the subject of a Care Order because her mother's current boyfriend had been physically and sexually abusing her. Amy has some behavioural problems in the class and has been anxious and distressed at times. However, she seemed to be settling into the nursery until a couple of weeks ago when she started to show signs of distress, wetting herself in class and being sulky and difficult. Today you found her crying at break and you asked her what the matter was. Amy told you that a 'bad man had hurt her down there'. She had difficulty speaking because she was very distressed. You asked Amy who the 'bad man' was and she said 'Daddy'. When you asked her who 'Daddy' was, Amy said Mr Smith.

1. Read the above scenario and decide what you would do next.
2. What would happen next?
3. What would happen to Amy in the short term?
4. Who might be be involved?

Compare your answers with those in Appendix II.

It is difficult in these circumstances to balance the rights of the child with the rights of the adult involved. However, if children are to be protected from all sources of abuse the possibility that a colleague might be involved in such abuse has to be considered. Your responsibilities do not change because the accused person is known to you. Talk the situation over with the appropriate person if you are in doubt about a colleague's behaviour with children.

Conclusion

Any adult working with children in any capacity has a responsibility to report suspicions or disclosures of child abuse to the child protection agencies. Young children may be totally reliant on childcare workers to initiate an investigation and to start the process by which abuse can be stopped. This may seem an enormous responsibility, but it is not one which you have to bear alone. Remember, if in doubt, take advice. You may fear reporting your suspicions and then finding them to be unfounded. However, if you do not report concerns then a child's safety and even life might be at risk.

Further Reading

Child Protection Procedures (available from local library).

DoH (1991) *Working Together under the Children Act 1989 – a Guide to Inter-agency Co-operation for the Protection of Children from Abuse*, London, HMSO. (To be replaced by *Working Together to Safeguard Children* in late 1998.)

5

The Legal Framework

Introduction

The whole of the child protection system is guided and controlled by legislation relating to the abuse of children. This legislation has changed over time in response to changes in ideas about and attitudes to child abuse. The role of legislation is to give powers and duties to those involved in child protection, and to provide them with the legal tools they need to act to protect children. The law also prevents those involved in child protection from abusing their power and acting without careful consideration or without evidence to support their belief that a child has been abused. Effectively, the law is there to ensure that the parent/child relationship can only be disrupted by the child protection process if there are clearly defined grounds for this to happen. From reading media reports about child protection, we could sometimes be forgiven for believing that social workers can act in the most arbitrary manner and that they have uncontrolled powers in respect of children. In fact, the action taken in respect of possibly abused children, without parental agreement, has to be approved by the courts. The courts have a role to listen to evidence and to decide whether or not to make an order in respect of a particular child.

It is unlikely that at this stage you will need to develop an in-depth knowledge and understanding of current childcare legislation. However, an awareness of the law relating to child protection may be helpful in understanding your own role and the corresponding role of other professionals in relation to child protection issues. It may be useful also when you are working with a child who is subject to a provision of the law, in helping you to understand the procedures that take place in respect of that child. In some circumstances you or your workplace may have responsibilities within the law towards children in your care. Some knowledge of the legal framework is helpful in clarifying the outcomes of child protection work, both for yourself, your colleagues, the child and her family.

A basic understanding of childcare legislation may help you to understand case conference procedures and recommendations, because the legislation effectively provides the framework within which professionals can act. For example, child protection social workers must act within the law when considering the removal of a child from her carers. As a child can only be removed from her carers if she is suffering harm as defined within the law, this will be the criterion which determines whether the removal takes place or not.

The current major piece of legislation affecting children and families in England and Wales at present is the Children Act, 1989. Before this Act was passed there were a number of pieces of legislation which governed the activities of child protection agencies and others involved in caring for children. However, these pieces of legislation were considered to be increasingly inadequate in providing effective child protection because they were complex, contradictory and in certain areas the provision was incomplete.

The Children Act, 1989, not only deals with child protection but also addresses many other areas of children's lives, for example arrangements for children after the divorce or separation of their parents. Our main concern is the parts of the Act that govern the lives of children and their families where abuse has taken place or is suspected to have taken place. This includes areas which govern the activities of social workers and the police in relation to how they would respond to information about possible abuse. However, we will also look at the provisions for children where abuse has taken place and legal action is taken in respect of the child, e.g. if the child is made the subject of a Care Order.

Principles of the Children Act, 1989

There are a number of general principles underlying the provisions within the Children Act. These effectively tell us what the legislation hopes to achieve in terms of the style and form of child protection provided. Part of the purpose in establishing these principles is to address some of the problems found in previous legislation. In particular, the Children Act, 1989, tries to emphasize that a child should only be made the subject of a court order if this is actually going to improve the child's situation. Similarly, delays in court action should be minimized in order to avoid children waiting for long periods of time for decisions to be made about their upbringing. In all circumstances, it is recognized that children are better off being cared for by their own families if this is possible. Obviously the child's welfare must come first and not all children can safely remain living with their own parents, but voluntary arrangements can be made with the agreement of all parties in some circumstances.

The Welfare Principle

One of the central principles underlying the provisions of the Children Act, 1989, is that the child's welfare should be 'paramount' in making decisions about her life and property. The idea of a welfare principle directing the court in its decisions is not new in the history of child care law. There is no definition within the Act to determine exactly what is meant by 'welfare' but it is clear that the term means a lot more than material and physical welfare and that it also refers to the child's emotional, social and moral well-being. The court must make decisions on the basis of the 'welfare principle' only when it has been satisfied that the child is or is likely to suffer significant harm, not just because it feels that the child would be better off living with different carers. Basically, this means that the court cannot just decide that a child would be better cared for in a different family. This option can only be considered if it is believed that the child is suffering or likely to suffer significant harm. In order that such decisions can be made by the court, there are a number of factors that should be taken into account when considering the child's welfare. These include:

- the wishes and feelings of the child (considered in the light of his age and understanding)
- the child's physical, emotional and educational needs
- the likely effect on the child of any change in his circumstances
- the child's age, sex and background and any characteristics of his which the court considers relevant
- any harm the child has suffered or is at risk of suffering
- how capable the parents or any other relevant person is of meeting the child's needs
- the range of powers available to the court.

By describing the child's welfare as 'paramount', the Act defines the basis on which the court can make a decision. Effectively, when all other considerations have been taken into account, the court must make a decision based on the child's best interests in terms of his welfare. This does not mean that other considerations like the wishes and feeling of parents or the wishes and feelings of the child himself will be ignored or put aside, but it does mean that the child's welfare is the overriding consideration.

Avoiding Delay

This principle rests on the belief that delay in dealing with child cases through the courts will have a detrimental effect on the child's welfare and therefore delays should be minimized to prevent them affecting the well-being of the child involved. Children who have to wait for court decisions about their lives and futures may miss out in the meanwhile on the stability and security that every child needs. In addition, the child's circumstances may change while this waiting takes place in ways which further complicate the decision-making process, e.g. if the child becomes attached to a foster carer during what was supposed to be a short-term placement. The courts are now required to draw up a timetable for care proceedings and supervision orders to prevent delays.

The Principle of Minimum Intervention

This refers to the requirement of courts to consider that a court order should only be made in respect of a child if it is better for the child to make an order than not. Effectively this means that the court must satisfy itself that an order will positively contribute to the child's needs being met and that the court should consider the outcomes of not making an order as well as making one. The underlying belief behind this principle is that children are better off being cared for by their families and that legal intervention should be avoided if at all possible. This principle is useful in that it makes the court consider not making an order in respect of the child as a positive option. It may be that there are different ways of meeting a child's needs which do not involve a court order, or that an order would not improve the child's situation.

Partnership

The Children Act, 1989, emphasizes the following points:

1. Local authorities should attempt to work in partnership with parents wherever possible.
2. There should be increased efficiency in the way in which the different agencies involved in child protection work liaise with each other and work together.

The first point relates to the need for local authorities to try and work with parents towards the best solution for the child and family, without resorting to the courts if at all possible. Children do not benefit if the proceedings to determine their lives and futures turn into a battlefield with parents on one side and social workers on the other. The Act tries to emphasize that it is possible to make agreements in some cases that do not involve complex legal procedures, and places the responsibility of trying to achieve this on local authorities. The idea behind this is to try and find a balance between protecting children and the avoidance of unnecessary interference in the lives of families. There is an implicit recognition within this that intervention can, in some circumstances, be harmful in itself. The Cleveland child abuse affair, which involved over 100 children, was one of the episodes which influenced this provision within the Act. The children were removed from their parents' care on suspicions of sexual abuse based on medical diagnosis. Among the other problems which arose were the complaints by parents that they were excluded from decision-making by the child protection agencies and that their relationships with their children were damaged by lack of involvement, lack of information and lack of contact.

The value of working in partnership with families is the prospect of better outcomes for the child and an increased respect for the rights of parents to be involved in decision-making about their family members. Although ultimately, some children are unable to continue living with their families safely, it is now felt that family involvement in the child protection process is in the best interests of the child.

Parental Responsibility

The idea of working in partnership with parents is underpinned by the concept of 'parental responsibility' which is introduced by the Children Act to replace the concept of parental rights which existed under previous legislation. The term 'parental responsibility' is defined as a concept which 'emphasises that the duty to care for the child and to raise him to moral, physical and emotional health is the fundamental task of parenthood and the only justification for the authority it confers' (DoH, 1991). The Act states that 'parental responsibility' is 'all the rights, duties, powers, responsibility and authority which by law the parent of a child has in relation to the child and his property'(Children Act, 1989, Section 3.1). Under the Children Act parents retain 'parental responsibility' for their children whatever orders the court might make in respect of the child, unless the child is actually adopted into another family. So, parents still retain 'parental responsibility' for children who are in care. Both parents share 'parental responsibility' for the child, including unmarried fathers who can share 'parental responsibility' with the mother, with her agreement. This sharing of 'parental responsibility' is not altered by divorce or separation, but can be limited by an agreement between the parents or a court order, e.g. where it is agreed or ordered that the child lives with one parent. The fundamental change brought about by the introduction of the concept of 'parental responsibility' is that the emphasis has moved away from the 'rights' of parents to the 'responsibilities' of parents. This change in emphasis has come about through the ever-increasing acknowledgement of children's rights (see Chapter 7). A further important change brought in by the Children Act is the sharing of 'parental responsibility' between parents and local authorities when a child is made the subject of a Care Order. This reflects the importance placed on the idea of working in partnership with parents, even when the child is looked after by the local authority.

Working Together: Inter-agency Co-operation

The arrangements for inter-agency co-operation in child abuse matters are laid out in the document *Working Together under the Children Act 1989* (DoH, 1991), prepared jointly by the Department of Health, the Home Office, the Department of Education and Science and the Welsh Office. (New guidelines, *Working Together to Safeguard Children*, will replace these in late 1998.) This document gives guidelines on how the various agencies involved in child protection can improve practice and how they can work more effectively together. This is partly in response to the findings of a number of child death enquiries in the 1980s which criticized the different agencies for not co-operating and working together in the best interests of the child. Lack of co-operation between agencies such as social services and health and education services was found to be a significant factor in the circumstances leading to the child's death in certain cases. *Working Together* offers guidelines to all agencies involved in child protection, reminding them of their duties and responsibilities, and laying down guidelines for how the different agencies should co-operate. Imagine that the various bits of information about a child are pieces of a jigsaw puzzle. If different professionals hold different pieces then it is vital that arrangements should be made for these to be shared in order to reveal the whole picture. *Working Together* also emphasizes that although confidentiality of information is vital, this should never be at the expense of child protection. *Working Together* states that 'Social workers and others working with a child and family must make clear to those providing information that confidentiality may not be maintained if the withholding of the information will prejudice the welfare of a child' (DoH, 1991, para. 3.15).

The inquiry into one particular child death highlighted the tragic consequences of poor inter-agency co-ordination and co-operation. Jasmine Beckford died in 1984 from multiple injuries inflicted by her stepfather. She had suffered injuries over a long period of time before her death. Despite the fact that Jasmine and her sister were subjects of Care Orders, Jasmine had rarely been seen by the social workers involved during the period before her death. In addition, she no longer attended the nursery place that had been found for her and the health visitor had not seen her for months. The inquiry report criticized the agencies involved on a number of counts, one of which was that liaison had been very poor and the whole picture had been obscured by lack of co-ordination of the information available about Jasmine's life and circumstances (DHSS, 1985).

Working Together lays out the responsibilities of different childcare professionals and agencies within the child protection procedures. In respect of your own roles the following is stated:

> Day nurseries, playgroups, out of school clubs and holiday schemes, and child minders, are likely to have an important part to play in helping parents under stress cope with their children's behaviour, to support them and give them a respite and thus prevent abuse. Local authorities will wish to ensure that all those providing such services and childminders are informed about what to do if they are concerned about a child. This should involve awareness training so that staff can recognise at an early stage the signs and behaviour which are a cause for concern. Day care providers in the private and voluntary sectors must have agreed procedures for contacting the local authority social services department about an individual child. (DoH, 1991, para. 4.41)

The guidelines go on to state that: 'Day care services and those provided by childminders are also crucial services for children at risk. By helping children directly and by monitoring their care at home, these services may be essential in helping a family remain together' (DoH, 1991, para. 4.42).

A Chance to Think

One of the biggest problems that arises when trying to make laws on the protection of children is how to balance the rights of families with the rights of the child. Families who experience a child protection investigation will obviously find this a traumatic event which disrupts their lives and creates a great deal of stress. However, without adequate powers available for possible abuse to be fully investigated, children will continue to suffer injury or even death at the hands of their parents.

Exercise 1

Think back over the last ten years, or as far as you can remember. What can you remember of reports in the media about child protection? Perhaps you can remember the Cleveland case, or the Orkneys case, or a number of cases where children died while under the supervision of the social services. Try and note down what impression you got of the activities of the professionals involved. Ask a friend or two what their memories are. You may find that your perception is that social workers and other professionals involved in these cases were heavily criticized for either intervening unnecessarily or for not intervening enough. Think about the difficulties of gaining a balance between protecting children from harm and avoiding unnecessary and possibly damaging intrusion into the lives of families.

Prevention of Abuse

The Children Act, 1989, gives local authority social services departments and others a range of duties and powers in respect of children who may be abused. The child protection provisions within the Act 'are designed to promote decisive action when necessary to protect children from abuse or neglect, combined with reasonable opportunities for parents, the children themselves and others to present their points of view' (DoH, 1991, p. 2).

The Act places the main responsibility for this on local authorities, although other professionals also have powers and duties in respect of children who may have been abused. In order to co-ordinate the efforts of different professionals, each area has an Area Child Protection Committee comprising senior representatives of the various agencies involved. One of the tasks of the committee is to produce the local Child Protection Procedures which describe the duties of different professionals working with children who may be abused, and the procedures which they should follow when abuse is known or suspected. The work of the ACPC and the purpose of the Child Protection Procedures are outlined in more detail in Chapter 4.

The local authority social services departments are given the duty, under the Children Act, to 'safeguard and promote the welfare of children within their area who are in need; and so far as is consistent with that duty, to promote the upbringing of such children by their families' (Children Act, 1989, Section 17). This provision clearly gives social services departments responsibility for providing services to help and support families as required in order to keep 'children in need' with their families if this is at all possible. Elsewhere, social services are given the duty to find out information about the needs of children in their area, on which to base the provision of these services. Within this general duty, social services departments also have the following additional duties:

- to take reasonable steps to prevent children in their area from suffering harm or neglect
- to take steps to reduce the need for care or supervision orders to be made in respect of children in the area

Local authority social services departments are therefore given duties to identify children who may be abused and to provide services to support these children and their families in order to make the children safer, as well as to reduce the need for children to come into care or be made the subject of a court order.

These provisions are in line with the general principle of the Act, that children should be brought up in their own families if at all possible. Social services departments are given these powers to try and prevent children being separated from their families through legal action. Not only can services be provided for the child in order to achieve a safer environment, but services can also be provided for other members of the family if this contributes to the protection of the child. For example, accommodation could be provided for the suspected abuser to move out of the family home to avoid the need for the child to be moved.

Other agencies are also involved in providing services to reduce the risk of harm to children, such as the health and education services and voluntary agencies. For families under stress the provision of such services may make the difference between serious child abuse occurring or not. In order to identify which children these preventative powers can be used with, we need to have some definition of a 'child in need'. One of the criticisms of the Children Act, 1989, is that the definition of the term 'children in need' is too vague, and therefore may be interpreted differently by different local authorities. However, the Act states that a child is in need if:

- the child is unlikely to achieve or maintain or to have the opportunity of achieving and maintaining a reasonable standard of health or development without the provision for him/her of services by a local authority;
- the child's health or development is likely to be significantly impaired or further impaired without the provision for him/her of such services; or
- the child is disabled. (Children Act, 1989, Section 17)

Some local authorities have published information about 'children in need' in their area and the sorts of services that could be offered to these children and their families.

The Children Act, 1989, heavily emphasizes the need for preventative work in respect of children and families in order to reduce the risk of harm and neglect to the children in those families. There is a clear purpose within the law to try and prevent abuse before it occurs or becomes serious. The sorts of services that could be offered are, for example, day care for under-5s, childminding, out of school care for older children, family centres, social work support advice and guidance, practical assistance in the home from a home help or home care aid and other activities to assist the children's development and alleviate stress within the family. There is a clear expectation that social services and other agencies will try and use such services to prevent abuse and alleviate stress in the family before they resort to legal action in respect of the child. Social services can call upon other agencies such as health and education services to make provision for children in need as required.

A Chance to Think

Working out which services can be offered to a child and her family in order to reduce the risks of abuse or neglect taking place can be a complex business for the workers concerned. Usually a representative of the social services department co-ordinates the various services provided by the different agencies in order to ensure that the help offered is sensible and that it works for the child and family. Obviously, any services to be offered must be acceptable to the child and family, and choices should be offered wherever possible. Another main consideration is cost. The Children Act, 1989, placed a lot of new responsibilities on local authorities and these all have cost implications. One of the concerns expressed about the change in legislation was whether local authorities would be able adequately to fund the provisions which now have to be made. Bear this in mind when doing the following exercise.

 Exercise 2

1. Things to do:

   • Obtain and read any information your local authority publishes on 'children in need' and the services available to them in your area.
   • Check if your library has a copy of *Working Together under the Children Act 1989* (or *Working Together to Safeguard Children* (1998) if available) which you can use for reference.

- Talk to colleagues about their understanding of what is meant by 'children in need'.

- Think about the children in your care. Do you think any of them would qualify as 'children in need'? Would any of them be eligible for services offered by your local authority to 'children in need'? Are you providing any of these services through your work role with a child?

- Remember to maintain confidentiality while doing this exercise.

2. Read the case study below. Do you think Amy is a 'child in need' and if so, why do you think this is so? What sort of services is Amy receiving to meet her needs already? What other services do you think might help Amy and her family? Compare your answers to the sample answers in Appendix II.

Amy is 3 years and 6 months old. She has had behavioural problems since being a young baby, which include chronic sleeplessness at night, prolonged screaming fits, aggressive behaviour towards other children and refusal of food. In addition, Amy has had delays in her speech development and she was late in walking and other physical developments. Amy seems to lack motivation to learn and she does not relate to other adults or children well. Amy's parents have found her a difficult and unrewarding child compared to her two older sisters. Her behaviour has caused a great deal of stress within the family and her parents have often quarrelled about how to deal with her tantrums and naughtiness. Amy has not been identified as a child with learning difficulties.

Social services became involved recently after a neighbour made an anonymous call to say that Amy was often beaten and locked in a bedroom for long periods of time. Bruises were found on Amy's arms and buttocks. Amy's father admitted to over-chastising her, but said he was at his wits end as to how to cope with her behaviour. Amy has been attending the nursery attached to the local infants school for three mornings a week for the past few weeks, but the teacher has already spoken to Amy's mother twice about her aggressive behaviour towards the other children.

Investigating Abuse

Every local authority has a duty to act upon information about the possible abuse of a child or children and to investigate that abuse. There are a number of different situations in which the local authority must investigate the circumstances of a child living in the area:

- when the child is suffering or is likely to suffer significant harm
- when there is an Emergency Protection Order in respect of the child or the child is in police protection
- when a court instructs the social services to make an investigation.

In this way local authority social services departments are given the prime responsibility for investigating possible abuse. However, it is quite clear that social services must make their investigation in conjunction with the other agencies involved with the child and family, and that other agencies will provide vital information for a full assessment of the child's situation and condition. Information can also come from members of the public, who may be involved in reporting the abuse in the first place. However, there is no legal requirement for any member of the public in the UK to report suspected abuse.

Significant Harm

The term 'significant harm' is used to define when legal intervention should take place in respect of children who may have been abused. 'Harm' is defined within the Act as 'ill-treatment or the impairment of health or development'.

1. 'Development' refers to physical, intellectual, emotional, social or behavioural development.
2. 'Health' includes physical and mental health.
3. 'Ill-treatment' includes sexual abuse and forms of cruel behaviour which are not physical.

The local authority must investigate abuse whatever the circumstances. This means that social services have to investigate possible abuse in foster homes and schools in the same way that any other suspected abuse would be investigated. The investigation should involve a thorough and widespread assessment of the child's condition and circumstances and should include consideration of whether legal proceedings under the Children Act, 1989, should be taken in respect of the child.

In addition to alerting other concerned agencies to be involved in the investigation, the social services department must inform the police if any offence has taken place. Local procedures will outline the way in which social services and the police should work together on child protection cases and in what circumstances a joint investigation may take place, e.g. serious physical injury or sexual abuse. The way in which child protection investigations are conducted is explored more fully in Chapter 4. The main point in respect of the legal framework is that the local authority social services departments have a duty to investigate cases of suspected abuse, and other agencies are obliged to assist in this process.

Emergency Protection Orders

There are a number of orders that the courts can make in respect of the child once an investigation has taken place. In most cases the removal of a child from her home will be carefully planned and organized to minimize distress to all parties. The social work profession and the police have been heavily criticized in the past for the dramatic and public removal of children from their homes in what have been often described by the media as 'dawn raids'. In *Working Together under the Children Act 1989* (DoH, 1991) it is emphasized that the timing of the removal of children from their homes should be considered very carefully to minimize the distress that such removal will cause to all parties. The timing has to be considered in the light of the need to protect the child, to preserve evidence, to arrest suspects and to cause the minimum distress to all involved. This will necessarily involve full consultation between the professionals involved to agree a suitable plan.

However, in some cases delay of any sort could be extremely harmful to the child and as such there is a provision for taking immediate action when a child is considered to be in 'acute physical danger' (DoH, 1991, para. 3). Before this provision is considered, however, other alternatives should be explored if they can be used to ensure the child's safety and avoid the need for legal intervention. These include assessing:

- whether a relative or other person could offer suitable care to the child
- whether the family will agree to the child being cared for by the local authority (accommodated)

• whether the person suspected of abuse will agree to leaving the home, possibly with the assistance of the local authority (see above).

If none of these alternatives is available or suitable, then an application for an Emergency Protection Order may be considered.

This order gives social workers and others the power to protect a child by removing her to a safe place, or keeping her in a safe place, if the risk to the child is serious at the time. The Emergency Protection Order (EPO) replaces what used to be known as a Place of Safety Order. Effectively, the EPO enables the applicant (the person who applies to the magistrate) to accommodate the child in a place he/she has chosen or to keep the child in such accommodation. This could be a hospital, a foster home or a residential centre for children. In theory, anyone can apply for an EPO, but usually the social services department will do so and then take responsibility for the order once it has been made. In practice, EPOs have by and large been made by child protection agencies.

An EPO can be made on the following grounds:

1. The child is likely to suffer significant harm if he is not moved to, or does not remain, in such accommodation.
2. The local authority is investigating the child's circumstances because they have reason to believe that the child is suffering, or will suffer, significant harm and access to the child is being unreasonably refused to the authorized person.

The EPO normally lasts for eight days but it can be extended for a further seven days. Courts will make the order if it is in the child's best interests to do so. Once the order is made the child can be kept in, or moved to, accommodation chosen by the applicant, e.g. a hospital or foster home. Parents can oppose the order after 72 hours have passed. When an EPO is made the court can also make directions for an assessment of the child, e.g. medical or psychiatric, and also regulate contact between the child and a 'named person'. This could be a parent or another person who the applicant felt should not have uncontrolled contact with the child, for example the person accused of the abuse.

In order to apply for an EPO the applicant must complete a detailed form, and take the application in front of a magistrate. Because the EPO is available to provide emergency protection to the child, magistrates are available in out-of-office hours to deal with applications. The social services emergency duty teams who deal with social work emergencies on evenings and weekends will have lists of magistrates on the out-of-hours rota. The order should only be made if the court is satisfied that the child is at risk of significant harm and also that there is no other way of achieving protection for the child. For example, the court will want to know why the child must be removed immediately and why this cannot be done with the parents' agreement and co-operation.

The order allows the applicant to enter certain premises to seek the child, and police help can be summoned if entry is refused. The applicant is advised to ask for this help and a warrant to gain entry at the time of applying for the EPO if problems in getting access to the child are predicted. The court can also order any person who knows where the child is to give this information to the applicant. During the period that the EPO is in force there should be reasonable contact allowed between the child and his parents or any others who he has been living with just before the order was made. The local authority may decide to restrict or supervise this contact and the court may make directions about contact with a specific person. In addition to the EPO, a police officer can take a child into 'police protection' for up to 72 hours, on the same grounds on which an EPO can be made.

The EPO is used mainly to protect children in emergency situations and some children may return to their homes after the order expires, or arrangements can be made for them in agreement with their parents. In some cases, however, the social services will begin care proceedings with an application for an interim Care Order and the child may well be on the way to becoming a child in care.

A Chance to Think

Removal from home is almost always going to be a distressing experience for a child. One of the principles of social work practice is that the additional trauma of intervention by the authorities should be kept to the minimum so that the child does not experience that intervention as further abuse. When a child must leave her home this raises many issues and problems. Where will she go to school? How will she see her friends and family members? Which toys, clothes and possessions will go with her? Who will know about her routines and her likes and dislikes? Who will understand her language for different needs? How will she explain what has happened to her?

Despite the abuse, many children will actively resist being removed from home because it is a fearful and emotionally painful experience.

Exercise 3

Read the case study below and make notes to show the steps the social worker might take to avoid having to apply for an Emergency Protection Order in respect of Winston. Describe the factors which might have to be taken into account in order to make a decision about how Winston can safely be cared for. Compare your answers with the sample answers in Appendix II.

Winston is 6 years old and lives with his parents and older sister. He comes from a large extended family, with both his maternal grandparents and his father's sister and her family living close by. Winston has been having problems in school since he started a year ago and you have been concerned about him. He is very withdrawn and does not concentrate well. Efforts to discuss problems with Winston's parents have met with little response. You have noticed that Winston is fearful of adults. Occasionally he has had minor facial injuries that he has not been able to explain. Today Winston arrived at school with a bruised eye and swelling to his jaw. He is moving stiffly and you feel that he has further injuries to his body. When questioned Winston says he fell. He becomes very upset and starts to cry. He says that he is scared to go home 'because his dad will be angry'. You call the social services and a duty social worker comes to see Winston in school.

Child Assessment Order

A Child Assessment Order (CAO) is made when there appears to be the need for a child to have an assessment of her physical or mental condition and this cannot be achieved in agreement with the parents. This provision was made within the Act to fill a gap perceived within the previous law. This gap was identified particularly in the report of the inquiry into the death of Kimberley Carlisle (DHSS, 1987). Among the factors which contributed to Kimberley's death was that the social services could not establish the level of risk to Kimberley because they could not get access to assess her.

Only the local authority or the NSPCC can apply for a CAO and the following grounds must be proved:

1. That the child is suffering or likely to suffer significant harm.
2. That an assessment of the state of the child's health or development or of the way in which he has been treated is required to enable the applicant to determine whether or not the child is suffering, or is likely to suffer significant harm.
3. That it is unlikely that such an assessment will be made, or be satisfactory, in the absence of a CAO.

The CAO is not an emergency order, but a planned response to concerns about the child's welfare. If the child is considered to be in danger of immediate harm then an EPO should be applied for instead. The CAO is more likely to be used where there are ongoing concerns about the child's health or development, and there has been no co-operation from the parents in investigating these concerns through an appropriate assessment. This could apply to children where neglect or sexual or emotional abuse are suspected, but no serious immediate risk is obvious. The assessment planned could be simple or complex, covering the child's development, sight, hearing, educational needs, physical or emotional condition. Assessments may be carried out by medical staff – doctors, specialists, child psychologists or psychiatrists, nurses or health visitors – or by social work staff, educational psychologists and others. The term 'assessment' is used very broadly to cover any aspect of the child's condition or behaviour that may be causing concern.

The order lasts seven days from the stated date when the assessment is to begin. The child can live away from home for up to seven days under this order to facilitate the assessment process, e.g. when the child must be a hospital in-patient in order to achieve the necessary assessment. The court can make directions both about the assessments planned and about the sorts of contacts the child will have during the period of the order. However, if the child is considered to have 'sufficient understanding to make an informed decision' the child may refuse the planned assessments. The court can also decide to make an EPO instead of a CAO if it is thought that there are sufficient grounds.

Although the CAO was seen as necessary to fill a gap in the legal options open to child protection agencies, in fact very few CAOs have been applied for since the Children Act, 1989, came into force. Perhaps parents do not continue to refuse an assessment for their child when they realize that legal action could be taken to enforce this. The fact that an EPO instead of a CAO could be made by the court may influence parents to co-operate, in case the court action results in the removal of their child from home.

Care Orders

Care Orders can be made in respect of children under 17. An order results in the child being placed in the care of the local authority which then assumes parental responsibility for the child. Parents still retain parental responsibility for the child, but it is now shared with the local authority. Only the local authority (social services) or the NSPCC can apply for a Care Order. The grounds for a Care Order are:

1. The child concerned is suffering significant harm, or is likely to suffer significant harm; and
2. The harm or likelihood of harm is attributable to
    (a) the care given to the child, or likely to be given tohim if the order were not made, not being what it would be reasonable to expect a parent to give to him; or
    (b) the child being beyond parental control.

The court will only make a Care Order if it is better for the child to do so. Before applying for an order, there must be full consultation between the agencies involved and with the child and the parents. This is usually done through the child protection case conference and should include a full assessment of the child and the ways in which her needs are being met or not met. It must be clear that no other suitable arrangements for the child can be made or that such arrangements have not met the child's needs. Obviously, making a Care Order in respect of a child is a very serious step affecting the whole of the child's future life and happiness. Such a step could never be taken lightly, or without every effort being made to help the parents to care properly for the child.

The important questions to resolve before a Care Order is made are to establish that the child was suffering significant harm, that this resulted from the parental care not being reasonable and that making a Care Order would be better for the child. In practice, these questions are difficult and complex and the courts often have to deal with a large amount of evidence before making a decision. It is by no means automatic that a Care Order will be made because the social services have applied for one. The court has the option of making an Interim Care Order which can last up to eight weeks in order to give the social services time to make a thorough investigation.

The local authority expected to promote contact between the child and his parents, other relatives and friends. If contact is thought to be undesirable, perhaps in the case of some children who have been abused, then the local authority can apply to the court to have contact with an individual or individuals denied. Contact may take place in a neutral place such as a foster home, a children's centre or a nursery, and contact may be supervised if this is thought necessary.

Care Orders last until the child is 18 years old unless there is a successful application for the discharge of the order before the child reaches this age.

Supervision Orders

Supervision orders can be made for one year or extended to three years if the local authority applies to the court for this to happen. Supervision Orders are made when there are concerns about the child's welfare which make supervision desirable, but where the concerns do not appear to warrant removal of the child from the care of his parents. The child is usually supervised by a social worker who has a duty to:

1. Advise, assist and befriend the supervised child.
2. Take such steps as are reasonably necessary to give effect to the order.
3. Consider whether or not to apply for discharge or variation where the order is no longer wholly complied with or may no longer be necessary.

The child who is supervised can be required by the supervisor to live in a specified place or to participate in specified activities, e.g. education and training. The supervisor can also require the person with parental responsibility for the child to ensure that he or she co-operates with the directions of the supervisor.

Residence Orders

A Residence Order can be made by the court to determine with whom a child is to live. Residence Orders can be made for a child to live with more than one adult, e.g. for the child to share her time between two parents. Parents or guardians can apply for a Residence Order, as can anyone with whom the child has lived for three years. Others can apply if they have the agreement of those with parental responsibility for the child, or the agreement of the local authority if the child is in care. For example, in a case where a mother had previously two children removed from her care because of physical abuse and neglect, it was decided by the case conference that her third child could not safely remain with her. A Care Order was made in respect of the baby. The mother's sister offered to care for the new-born baby, and eventually she applied for a Residence Order in respect of the child with the agreement of the local authority.

The Child in Legal Proceedings

You might be forgiven for thinking after reading the above that the child is seen as a pawn in the legal system, to be moved at the will of concerned adults. Indeed, this has been one of the features of child protection in the courts in the past. The Children Act, 1989, has made attempts to address the issue of children's rights by increasing the provisions by which the child's own views and opinions will be heard. There have been recent changes to help children take a part in court proceedings, and a much more serious approach to listening to what the child wants.

The Children Act makes it obligatory to ascertain and take into account the child's wishes and feelings about where she will live and who she will live with. Obviously, the extent to which this can be done depends on the age and maturity of the individual child. Taking the child's wishes and feelings into account does not mean making decisions based solely on what the child says she wants. If the child's welfare and the child's wishes conflict, the child's welfare must be the most important consideration. Listening to the child has to be part of the decision-making process, not the whole of it. Children involved in court proceedings will normally have an independent social worker appointed to represent their interests. These independent social workers are called 'guardians *ad litem*'. A guardian has extensive duties to investigate the circumstances of the child, and to compile a report for the court in which the child's best interests are represented.

In response to an increasing awareness of the child's rights there have been changes in the way children are viewed as witnesses. The assumption that young children cannot give truthful, accurate accounts of events has now been challenged, and there is an increasing belief that even quite young children can make good witnesses. Research has shown that children are unlikely to lie about abuse, or give a false account of events. The main influence on whether children tell the truth or not is that of adult suggestion. Techniques for interviewing children who have been abused have been greatly developed in the 1990s to help those involved in disclosure to avoid leading the child into false allegations.

One of the main problems in successfully prosecuting child abusers has been the need for the child to give evidence in court. This has been particularly problematic in cases of sexual abuse where there are often no other witnesses and little material evidence to corroborate the child's story. For many children, younger and older, the ordeal of having to give evidence against a parent or someone close to them, with that person present in the court, has been quite impossible to undergo. Even without the painful nature of the evidence, and the intimidating aspects of the court itself, children are overwhelmed by the responsibility placed on them in this situation. Since 1988 it has been possible for children to give evidence in court via a video link which precludes the need for the child to be present in court. Research has shown that this has benefited children by reducing the distress experienced during the giving of evidence (Davies and Noon, 1990).

Some would argue that children are now believed at all costs on the subject of abuse and that this has made the task of parents and childcare workers hazardous. Some childcare workers have expressed the concern that they are vulnerable to false accusations. Parents, particularly fathers, have argued that they place themselves open to allegations of child abuse simply by performing ordinary childcare tasks such as bathing. However, the balance between the rights of children and the rights of adults has to be achieved so that protection of children can take place effectively.

Conclusions

Learning about childcare legislation gives you some idea of the boundaries within which the child protection process takes place and the expectations that are placed on the child protection agencies. Your own role in this may be quite limited in terms of direct involvement with the courts. However, you may have a great deal of information to supply to the process, and a role in the care and monitoring of a child at risk. You may also find it helpful to recognize where the child is within the legal process as you may well be supporting the child during the difficult period of investigation and its outcomes.

References

Children Act (1989) London, HMSO.

Davies and Noon (1995) 'An Evaluation of the Live Link for Child Witnesses', in C. Cobley (ed.) *Child Abuse and the Law*, London, Cavendish, p. 164.

DoH (1991) *Working Together under the Children Act 1989*, London, HMSO.

DHSS (1985) *A Child in Trust; Jasmine Beckford* (The Jasmine Beckford Report), London, HMSO.

DHSS (1987) *A Child in Mind; Protection of Children in a Responsible Society* (The Kimberley Carlisle Report), London, HMSO.

Further Reading

Adcock, M., Hollows, A. and White, R. (1993) *Child Protection Update*, Northampton, Greenshires (for the National Children's Bureau).

Lyon, C. and de Cruz, P. (1993) *Child Abuse*, Bristol, Jordan.

6

Working with Children Who May Have Been Abused

Introduction

A child who is suspected or known to have been abused is usually the subject of a child protection investigation, as outlined in Chapter 4. The child may also be subject to legal proceedings which may involve her removal from home to other carers or supervision in his own home. A child who is thought to have been abused will have been the subject of a case conference which makes recommendations about the child's future, which may change her life. The child protection investigation may involve interviews with social workers and with the police. The child's testimony may have been recorded on video and the child may be given a medical examination in order to collect forensic evidence. All this activity will be aimed at establishing whether abuse has taken place and at preventing any repetition. It may also result in a prosecution against the abuser.

By now you may be quite rightly thinking, 'But, what about the child? Where are her needs and feelings being considered in all this?' This chapter aims to look at the effects on the child herself rather than at the procedural and legal response to suspected abuse. A child who discloses abuse or is discovered to be abused will normally become the centre of a complex procedure which may, if the adults involved are not careful, manage to overlook the child herself. It may seem sometimes that discovering the truth and protecting the child are the be-all and end-all of the child protection process. In fact, the investigation is only the beginning. The child will have many needs apart from protection, which must also be dealt with. For many children, the end of the investigation may be the beginning of some help for them personally. This might be because the efforts of the professionals have focused on what might be a complex and difficult investigation, or because work with the child on how he feels may be postponed in case it 'muddies' the evidence which will be presented in court. Whatever the reason, many children who have been abused will need a good deal of additional help in coping with what has happened to them.

The investigation, however sensitively handled, may be highly traumatic for the child, adding to the distress and misery caused by the abuse. Although there is no suggestion that abuse should not be investigated in case the child is further distressed, it is important to be aware that the child will not always experience the investigation in the same way as do the adults involved. Most young children have only the vaguest idea about the possible outcomes of the disclosure of abuse. Many abused children just want the abuse stopped, and everything else in their lives to remain the same. The child may love the abuser, even if they hate the abuse, and will consequently feel upset and guilty if the discovery of the abuse results in the abuser being prosecuted or made to leave home. It may be hard for the child to understand the adult reasoning behind decisions made about his future and those decisions can sometimes feel more like punishment than help to the child. It is important to remember that the investigation itself may be a traumatic experience for the child. During the investigation the child's daily routine may change or remain the same. Whichever happens the child will need a great deal of support and understanding from his day-to-day carers in order to cope with the changes and uncertainties that are happening to and around him. A child may get a lot of this support at home but, if the discovery of abuse has disrupted family life, it is possible that the child's needs could be overlooked while the adults around the child struggle with their own problems.

The effects of abuse on young children can be many and varied and may manifest themselves in a variety of ways. Children respond differently to abuse and the response of a particular child will depend on a whole range of complex and interrelated factors such as the extent and duration of the abuse, the type of abuse, the relationship with the abuser, the response from other significant adults, and the personality of the child himself. We cannot, therefore, state precisely how a child will react to having been abused. However, there are certain generalizations that can be made about the effects of abuse on children, and how we might expect the child to respond.

In this chapter we will explore the possible long- and short-term consequences of different types of abuse on children and the behaviours which may result. We will look at how to handle difficult behaviour sensitively and effectively, and how we can help the child restore or build self-esteem and self-confidence through everyday contact with the child and also by the use of specific techniques to help her work through feelings and emotions. We will consider how to involve parents in this process and help them help their child. It is important to remember that there are no 'magic solutions' for the child and that working through the consequences of child abuse can be a long and slow process. Some children who have suffered through abuse will be offered specialist therapy or counselling to help them recover, but this will still leave an important role for those who care for the child on a day-to-day basis.

The consequences of severe abuse can be lifelong for children who do not receive help and sympathetic support at an early stage. Many adults ask for help with abuse which happened in their childhood when they come to realize that the abuse is still affecting their lives, relationships and happiness. It is crucial to offer the child the help that she needs at an early stage, in order to minimize the long-term effects of abuse. Although it may be a difficult and long process, the rewards are profound – helping a child to be happy and enjoy life again.

Finally, it is important to remember that each child is an individual with her own needs and feelings and her own personality, identity and culture. There can be no prescriptions for how to work with every child. However, there are guidelines which may be helpful, although much of your work will be based on your own knowledge and experience of that particular child.

A Chance to Think

 The effects of abuse are complex and far-reaching in a child's life, often impairing the child's ability to develop skills and abilities, to make relationships that are positive and fulfilling and to build the inner strengths and self-confidence we all need. It is important not to underestimate just how profound the effects of abuse can be on a child and how they can influence every aspect of the child's growth and development.

Exercise I

Before reading the next section, try and make a list summarizing what you think might be the possible effects of child abuse in terms of the child's physical and emotional well-being and behaviour. Look back at Chapters 2 and 3 to remind yourself of the different types of abuse if necessary. Read through the next section and compare your list with the 'Summary of the Possible Effects of Abuse' at the end of the section.

The Effects of Child Abuse

The effects of child abuse are summarized in the chart on page 121.

Physical Effects

The immediate effects of physical abuse can range from minor injuries such as bruising, through to broken bones and internal injuries. Although children may suffer terribly from horrific physical injuries, many heal with barely a scar. However, for a small proportion of children physical abuse can result in permanent injury or death. One example of this is the result of a subdural haematoma (bleeding of the membrane surrounding the brain) which can cause permanent brain-damage or death. This injury can be caused in young children and toddlers by shaking or throwing the child. Physical abuse can also result in developmental delays relating to the child's mental and physical growth. This can lead to short- or longer-term learning delays which may become apparent at school or nursery. Although there may be actual physical causes for these delays, for example if the child has had time off school through illness or injury, they are often attributed to the emotional and psychological effects of abuse.

Children who have been physically abused and/or neglected may grow up in severely deprived conditions. This may result in poor physical growth which may be apparent in the child's height and weight, vulnerability to illness and disease, and a general appearance of lack of health and care. In some children this causes a syndrome known as 'failure to thrive', which results in delayed growth, poor appearance with sparse dry hair and splotched purplish skin, developmental delays, and a child who may have 'infantile proportions' to the body long after the age where the body shape should have elongated and changed as the child grows out of the toddler stage. Children who 'fail to thrive' often show dramatic developmental improvements when moved to a different care environment.

The results of neglect may be more vague and difficult to define, however. Neglected children may suffer less dramatic impairment of their growth and development, which still may affect weight, height, motor skills and learning ability. Neglected children may also suffer from untreated illnesses, such as hearing impairment caused by ear infections. These children may also show signs of malnutrition and vitamin deficiencies which may affect the child's lifelong health chances.

The effects of sexual abuse of children are often seen primarily as emotional and behavioural. However, sexually abused children may suffer physical injury to the genitals and anus if penetration has taken place, and the child may also contract sexually transmitted diseases from the abuser or become pregnant. Young children who have been sexually abused may have to be tested to discover their HIV status, if the abuser is HIV-positive or has AIDS.

Emotional and Behavioural Effects

A child who lives in an unpredictable and unsafe environment may develop an almost uncanny ability to detect the state of mind of her abuser. This ability is developed as a defence mechanism by which the child hopes to avoid further abuse by not provoking anger, or acting to placate the aggressor. For these children there is no 'time off' – they live in a constant state of tension, waiting for the next blow to fall. Such children have been described as being in a state of 'frozen watchfulness' where they do as little as possible to provoke abuse, while constantly watching the abuser in order to try and pre-empt a further attack. These children may become very skilled at meeting adult needs at an early age, as they strive to understand what exactly triggers an attack. These children may respond to other adults in the same way, impairing their ability to make real relationships.

Children who are subject to physical aggression often become aggressive themselves, usually towards other children. This may be because attacking other children releases the frustration and anger that a young child can feel when the subject of abuse. It can also be because the child has learned that this is a way of dealing with other humans that is effective in terms of getting his own way. Children who suffer sexual abuse can also become physically and sexually aggressive to other children.

A young child who is sexually abused by an adult may learn to relate to other adults in a sexual way, because this is how she has learned to please 'grown-ups'. This can be extremely disconcerting for those other adults, and may well make the child vulnerable to further abuse. For example, a 4-year-old girl taken into care because she had been sexually abused by a number of adult males horrified her new foster father by unzipping his fly and attempting to masturbate him. His revulsion was obvious and the child was left feeling bewildered and rejected. From her point of view, she had been relating to the foster father as she had been taught to relate to all adult males. An older child may become promiscuous with both peers and adults, as he or she seeks to please others or gain affection through sexual activities.

Emotional abuse, which often results from other types of abuse, can lead to low self-esteem and poor self-confidence. The child may have little sense of self through being denied basic love and care, through being treated as an object, denied the right to have needs, views and opinions of his own, and perhaps being made to feel that he deserves the treatment that he has received. Children who are sexually abused are often made to feel valueless because they are denied the right to make choices about the most intimate parts of themselves. This lack of self-esteem can be one of the longer-term effects of abuse, lasting throughout adulthood and affecting all aspects of life.

Emotional abuse can also lead to disruptive and damaging behaviour aimed at those around the child. This may involve angry, defiant behaviour, refusal to obey instructions, damage to property and attacks on others. Some children, however, may behave very differently, and become withdrawn, indifferent and depressed. All abuse involves the child in high levels of stress, and this may result in strange or bizarre behaviour, regressive behaviour where the child returns to the behaviour patterns of a younger age, or self-destructive behaviour where the child attempts to harm herself. This may also include eating and sleeping problems, bed-wetting, outbursts and tantrums.

Perhaps the most serious long-term consequence of abuse is the effect it may have on the child's ability to make relationships in childhood and later life. Children who have been abused from an early age may never have received the positive loving care needed in order to make attachments to their carers. These children may then have great difficulty in knowing how to make loving, trusting relationships later in life, because they have not had this experience themselves during the crucial early years.

For many children the damage caused by abuse can be overwhelmingly frightening. The child may feel that he cannot recover from the experiences that he has had. This may result in depression or recklessness where the child seems not to care what happens to him.

Summary of the Possible Effects of Abuse

- Short- or long-term impairment to health, growth and development including learning ability.
- Aggressive behaviour including bullying, fighting and verbally abusive behaviour.
- Sexually aggressive behaviour towards other children, inappropriately sexual behaviour towards adults.
- Loss of confidence, low self-esteem and poor self-image.
- Difficult behaviour including wetting and soiling, disruptive behaviour, tantrums and outbursts, refusing to respond to requests.
- Unhappiness, sadness, withdrawal and listlessness.
- The development of obsessive or compulsive behaviour, e.g. self-mutilation, rituals, bizarre behaviour.
- Fear of adults.
- Attempts to ingratiate with adults by offering affection indiscriminately, or making superficial relationships at an early stage.

Working through the Effects of Abuse

When a child has been abused this may produce a wide range of emotions and feelings in response. The child may need opportunities to work through these feelings in order to begin the healing process. For many children the fact of being abused has been hidden or a secret. It may be that after the abuse has come into the open, the child may need to deal with feelings that have been suppressed for a long time. The child may also have feelings about the investigation of his abuse, especially if that investigation has resulted in changes in the child's circumstances. Most young children want the abuse to stop, but otherwise want life to remain the same. They may love the abuser and not wish to be separated from him or her. Although each child has her own individual reactions to being abused these are some of the feelings a child may have:

- anger towards the abuser
- anger towards other adults who may have supported the abuse or ignored the fact that the abuse was taking place
- shame, self-blame or guilt, in that the child feels responsible for the abuse taking place
- guilt that the abuser may be suffering through disclosure
- guilt about the possible or actual breakdown of the family as a result of the abuse being discovered
- in the case of sexual abuse, the child may feel guilty about enjoying the activities she has been involved in
- confusion about what should happen in families, as opposed to what has happened
- anxiety and fear about the future
- in some cases fear that the abuser will be allowed to abuse again
- sadness, depression and despair
- feelings of being unloved or, even, hated
- helplessness and lack of control.

Some of these feelings may be expressed through difficult behaviour. This should indicate to the worker that painful feelings exist and need to be dealt with. Obviously, for the sake of the child and others around her the behaviour must first be dealt with. This is discussed in the next section. However, as well as dealing with the behaviour sensitively, you also need to deal with the feelings that lie behind the behaviour. Some children will not express their feelings through behaviour. The child who suppresses her emotions about the abuse may need more structured opportunities to express her feelings during her day-to-day routine. The child may find her feelings very hard to cope with particularly if they are powerful negative emotions. The child may be actively afraid of expressing highly destructive feelings because she fears the outcome. She may also fear that these very destructive emotions may damage you or other adults if they are expressed openly.

It may seem easier for both worker and child if these negative emotions remain suppressed. However, it is in the expression of these feelings that the healing process starts for the child. Left unexpressed they may cause long-term damage to the child's ability to make trusting relationships and to develop self-confidence and a positive view of self.

Some abused children who are in your care may receive ongoing individual therapeutic help from a social worker, a child psychologist, a child psychiatrist or a play therapist. In some local authorities there are special centres for children with difficulties, sometimes called Child Guidance Centres. These are usually staffed by child psychologists and sometimes specially trained social workers. There may also be family therapy workers who work with the whole family to try and help them function better as a unit. Often the case conference will have recommended the child should be referred for this sort of help and, depending on availability, the child may receive it. If this is the case, there may be a care plan which details the type of help the child should receive. It is helpful if your role is clarified with other workers involved with the child, so that the help offered to the child is consistent and effective.

Dealing with Difficult Behaviour

Difficult behaviour may be the first indication that a child in your care has been abused. It is also often the first effect of abuse that you have to deal with. Although a child's behaviour may be affected by many different factors, e.g. divorce, bereavement or the birth of a sibling, abuse is always a possible explanation (see Exercise 3 in this chapter). Children who have been abused may try and show their unhappiness through their behaviour because they do not have the words to describe what is happening to them, or because they are afraid to talk about the abuse. However, the discovery and investigation of abuse may not necessarily result in improved behaviour. The investigation and the outcomes of the decision-making process about the child's future may be a bewildering and distressing experience for the child, particularly if it results in him being parted from those that he loves.

You might be working with the child throughout the whole process, from when suspicions of abuse began to arise through to the aftermath of the child protection process. The child will be under a great deal of stress and this may show in her behaviour and attitude towards others. Possible behavioural problems have been outlined above, but clearly it is important to remember that each child's reaction will be unique.

Sheila was 5 years old when she was found, along with her two younger brothers, and a brother and two sisters in their teens to have been sexually abused by her uncle. The abuse had been a closely kept family secret for many years and only came to light when Sheila's oldest sister left home, and told her social worker what was happening in the family. Both Sheila's parents knew about the abuse and apparently condoned it. Sheila's older brother, who had been abused from early childhood himself, was involved with his uncle in the abuse of his younger sister and brothers. All the children were removed from home, but could not be found placements together. Sheila was placed on her own with foster carers.

Sheila had been at school for four months before the abuse was disclosed. During that time, her teachers had expressed concern on several occasions about her attitude and behaviour. Apparently Sheila failed to make friends at school and was withdrawn and distant in her manner. She did not join in the usual play at breaks, but had on two occasions instigated some worrying 'secret' play in the toilets, which involved among other things trying to poke a stick into the genitals of other girls. When this was discussed with her she became extremely agitated and upset, denied the game had taken place, and on one occasion become almost hysterical in her denials.

Sheila showed aptitude at her lessons, but was uncooperative and sometimes rude, bad-mannered and unpleasant in her attitude to teachers and pupils. Her teachers and foster carers found Sheila difficult to became fond of. Her withdrawn manner and rather sly, knowing attitude were not endearing. In particular the foster father reported that he felt uncomfortable around Sheila, who seemed to regard him with hatred at times. Her behaviour in the foster home was characterized by withdrawal and lack of cooperation. When pressed to respond she would sometimes have hysterical outbursts, screaming abuse and lashing out at anyone who came near her. These outbursts would be followed by profound withdrawal, during which Sheila made no response to anything around her.

Sheila was made subject of a Care Order and began therapy to help her express her feelings about the abuse. The therapy helped her talk about her feelings of anger about what had happened to her, and helped her also to explore her lack of trust of adults. Eventually, Sheila was able to make relationships with her foster carers, and at school, although this was a slow process which took a long time.

A Chance to Think

In theory we probably feel that we would have an enormous amount of compassion and sympathy for an abused child. In practice, the behavioural problems an abused child may develop can make day-to-day care an extremely difficult and unrewarding task. The case study above demonstrates some of the issues that may arise.

Exercise 2

1. If you were Sheila's teacher how do you think you should have reacted to discovering the 'secret' game? What sort of reactions would be (a) helpful (b) unhelpful? Draw up a list.
2. Imagine you are Sheila's foster father. How would you have tried to behave towards Sheila? Draw up a list of 'dos' and 'do nots'.
3. If you were Sheila's foster mother how would you try and cope with Sheila's hostility towards your husband?
4. What concerns might the foster carers have if they had younger children in their family? How might they have tried to deal with these concerns?

Compare your answers to the sample answers in Appendix II.

Caring for a child who has been abused can be a difficult and demanding task. You may not have all the information you need in order to understand the child's feelings and you may not understand why the social workers are not sorting matters out more speedily. You may be caring for a number of children and have concerns about the effect of one child's behaviour on the group. Parents of other children may be complaining about the abused child's behaviour towards their children or the influence that behaviour has on their children. You may be dealing with hostility or aggression from the abused child's parents, especially if you were involved in reporting the abuse. In the middle of this you may have an unhappy, distressed child to deal with who manifests her feelings through difficult and challenging behaviour.

In the next box are a number of guidelines for dealing with difficult behaviour. Of course it would need an angel to display this level of patience, tolerance and calm all the time, but the guidelines are there as an indicator of the sort of responses it can be helpful to consider when faced with difficult behaviour. Read through them and see if there are any you would like to add. Think also about why it might be hard for you to follow these guidelines at times – what will get in the way in your particular job role and circumstances?

Coping with Difficult Behaviour

1. Stay calm and cool.
2. If the child becomes difficult or aggressive try and get him on his own, away from other children.
3. Only physically restrain the child if his behaviour is dangerous to himself or others. Be gentle.
4. If you are losing your temper, take time out briefly.
5. Talk to the child about her feelings, and why the behaviour occurs.
6. Set boundaries and be consistent about them.
7. Be dependable and reliable in the child's life so he can learn to trust you and see you as constant.
8. Praise and reward the child when her behaviour is 'good'.
9. Distinguish between the child and the behaviour and let the child know that you still care about her even if you do not like how she is behaving.
10. Never threaten a child, or try and belittle her. Try and show the child how to behave through your own consistency, politeness and respect for others.
11. Never pretend that the abuse did not happen, or tell the child that it is in the past. The experiences the child has had may take a long time to work through, and the child needs to resolve his own feelings in his own time.
12. Get some support for yourself in order to deal with your own feelings.
13. Distract the child into other activities.
14. Help the child to develop alternative behaviours through praising more acceptable behaviour and giving the child alternative suggestions as to how she might respond in different situations.

Children who are abused need help with difficult behaviour, not just because it is unpleasant for other people to cope with, but because such behaviour can be self-destructive. The child may 'prove' to himself that he is unacceptable and undeserving by alienating other children and adults with his expressions of anger and despair. A child who becomes self-destructive in this way may carry these problems into adolescence and adulthood. Children who have been abused desperately need to feel that they are worthy and valuable in themselves. Some difficult behaviour may be 'testing out' – 'will you still love me even if I'm horrible?' The child may need constant reassurance that he is valued, and may try and present himself in the worst possible light in order to see if the adult will still care about him. Children who have been rejected may seek further rejection as a confirmation of their unworthiness.

A Chance to Think

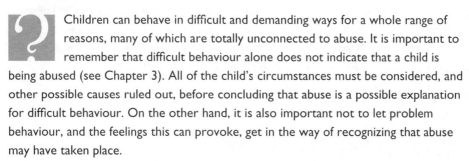

Children can behave in difficult and demanding ways for a whole range of reasons, many of which are totally unconnected to abuse. It is important to remember that difficult behaviour alone does not indicate that a child is being abused (see Chapter 3). All of the child's circumstances must be considered, and other possible causes ruled out, before concluding that abuse is a possible explanation for difficult behaviour. On the other hand, it is also important not to let problem behaviour, and the feelings this can provoke, get in the way of recognizing that abuse may have taken place.

Exercise 3

Look back at Exercise 2 in Chapter 3 and read your notes and the relevant sample answers in Appendix II again, to remind yourself of the range of possible explanations for difficult behaviour in a child.

Trust is hard to rebuild with children who have not been able to trust those who should have cared for them most. The child may develop a general distrust of adults, and this may make the relationship with the child difficult to establish and/or sustain. Some children who have been abused may express their insecurity through clinginess, attention-seeking and demanding behaviour. These children may rapidly make superficial relationships with adults around them, and present as loving and caring. However, the relationship may be 'unreal' in that the child is attempting to please, rather than establishing a genuine rapport.

An extreme example of this is Sandra, who by the age of three was a very insecure little girl due to repeated rejections by her mentally ill mother, who sometimes failed to provide the most basic care. Sandra would ask any adult female who paid her any attention if she could go home with her and would tell the adult that she loved her, in a desperate attempt to gain some love and security.

Lack of self-esteem and poor self-confidence, combined with behavioural problems and possibly developmental delays, may result in a child who can easily be labelled as a problem. It is important that we remember that the problem is not the child himself, but the adult behaviour that caused the damage in the first place. Young children and some children with learning disabilities may have long-term problems in simply understanding what has happened to them. However, children may experience feelings about being abused and respond to those feelings, even if they do not fully understand what has caused them.

One of the main problems that children who have been abused suffer from is lack of self-esteem and feelings of worthlessness and self-blame. These feelings can, in some cases, last a lifetime unless help and support are offered to the child to aid her recover her confidence and sense of belonging. The next section explores how childcare workers who have regular contact with an abused child can contribute to this process.

Helping the Child Gain Self-esteem

Before you can help the child to restore or gain self-esteem, the child must be able to learn to trust you. The child will not be able to do this unless he sees you as 'trustworthy'. So, what do we mean by 'trustworthy'?

- Showing warmth, acceptance and support.
- Being honest and truthful with the child.
- Consistency.
- Respecting the child's point of view, non-judgemental.
- Giving of self.

The child needs to develop confidence in your reliability, and in your ability to cope with her feelings and behaviour. Often children will test out those closest to them in order to establish their trustworthiness. This means sometimes that the child's behaviour will be worst with those she feels closest to and has most confidence in. However, establishing your own trustworthiness is vital in making a relationship with the child. Many children who have been abused find it hard to make real relationships with adults. They might shy away from such relationships altogether, or make superficial relationships with the adults around them. In helping the child to make a relationship with you, you are contributing to helping the child restore this ability in general.

When the child has started to learn to trust you, and has begun to become involved in a relationship with you, then you may be able to help the child to restore lost self-esteem. By self-esteem we mean the ability to value ourselves and see ourselves as important and worthwhile human beings. Children develop self-esteem through a growing knowledge of self, reflected back from significant others – usually parents and other caretakers. The child will start to see himself as others see him through a process of recognizing how others respond to him. For example, a child who is given praise and approval when he has done well, who might receive appropriate punishment for unacceptable behaviour, but is not constantly criticized, who is told that he is loved, wanted and important, and whose needs are met by those around him, will develop a positive view of himself as valuable and important. His self-esteem will be good.

A child who is constantly 'put down', criticized, belittled, and denied the right to have even her most basic needs met will develop a negative view of herself, seeing herself as worthless and unimportant. Her self-esteem will be poor.

Children who have been abused have often been denied the right to have even their most basic needs met and so have had little chance to develop their own sense of self-worth. For many of these children the outcome is chronically poor self-esteem. Obviously this depends on the extent and nature of the abuse, and the relationship the child had to the abuser, but most children who have been abused will have suffered some damage to their sense of self-worth.

A Chance to Think

 Children have many and varied needs which have to be met in order that the child can develop into a happy, contented and achieving human being. The child learns about himself from the adults around him, by the extent to which they are able to meet his needs.

Exercise 4

1. List the types of needs a child may have, and compare your list to the sample at the beginning of Appendix II.

2. Think of the children you care for and identify which of these types of needs you are involved in meeting. You will almost certainly be meeting the child's basic physical needs, but which other types are important in your own work setting?

3. Read the example below.

   (a) Which of John's needs do you think are not being met by his parents?

   (b) Do you think he might be getting any of these needs met elsewhere?

   (c) What feelings do you think John might have about himself?

   (d) How could John's foster carers help John with these feelings?

Compare your answers with the sample answers in Appendix II.

Example

John was 9 when he was taken into care after a long period of concern about possible abuse by his parents. John's mother found it difficult to love her son, who was the unwanted child of a very unstable and violent relationship. John's father dominated the family with his violent temper and his belief that boys should be tough. John was excessively punished for minor misdemeanours, either by being shut in his room without food for long periods, or by being hit with a belt. If he cried or became upset he was belittled and laughed at by his father, and called a 'girl' and a 'pansy'. Although John's schoolwork was good, this was not recognized as an achievement by his parents who were suspicious of an education that they had not benefited from themselves.

John received no praise, very little love and as such did not develop a positive sense of self. He saw himself as useless and unsuccessful, and was beginning to have doubts about his own masculinity which confused and frightened him. Work with the family failed to help them see the damage that was being done to John. The father maintained that his child-rearing practices would 'make a man' of John. The father claimed that he had been raised in this way by his own father and that this had not harmed him and therefore would not harm John. John went to live in a foster home. The foster carers found John to be anxious and withdrawn, with few responses to his environment and a sad, unhappy air about him.

Before we look at how to help a child restore self-esteem we need to look at how we might recognize the signs of poor self-esteem in a child. Children react in different ways to lack of care, so there are no hard and fast rules for recognizing poor self-esteem. However, if we know that a child has been abused then this should indicate the possibility of lack of self-worth and low self-confidence.

A child who has been abused may well blame herself for the abuse taking place. Many children believe that it is something that they have done which causes the abuse to happen, or a characteristic that they possess which invites abuse. A child who has been sexually abused may blame herself for not resisting or saying no. Some of these children have totally unrealistic views of the sort of things they could have done to resist the abuser. Perhaps one of the most important messages the child needs to receive throughout the whole child protection process is that she was not at fault, and that the fault lies with the abuser. It can be very hard to substantiate this message to children when the abuser does not receive any punishment. Sexually abused children in particular may be confused at a message that tells them that the abuser is to blame, and then allows that abuser to walk free.

Children who have been subject to racist abuse may blame themselves for being black and become hostile to their own culture and race. This could mean focusing feelings of anger on themselves in a destructive way. These children may see evidence of racism all around them and experience discrimination on a daily basis, but see no evidence that the abusers are to be punished or prevented from behaving in this way.

A child with low self-esteem may exhibit some of the following characteristics and behaviour:

- withdrawn, unresponsive behaviour
- depression or sadness
- lack of enjoyment in the activities he is involved in
- lack of confidence in approaching new tasks or situations
- anxiety or panic
- feelings of failure or inability to achieve
- low expectations of self
- refusal to try new tasks or activities
- anger or aggression when faced with new tasks or situations
- lack of self-care
- self-harming or reckless behaviour.

It can be difficult to help a child build self-esteem and self-confidence, especially a child who has never had the opportunity to develop good feelings about herself. However, on a day-to-day basis there are many things which can be done to help. Perhaps the most important thing you can do is to show the child that you genuinely care about her, through warmth, sincerity and consistency in your behaviour and manner towards her. The child will need to be praised for achievements and successes, and acceptable behaviour should be encouraged by reinforcing the child's good feelings with praise and rewards.

Look at the checklist below and think what ways to improve a child's self-esteem you could add to the list. Which of these methods of helping would be suitable in your work setting with the children you care for?

Helping the Child to Improve Self-esteem

1. Showing positive regard for the child – affection, warmth and respect.
2. Being consistent with the child – setting limits and boundaries and maintaining them. Children can derive a great deal of security from knowing how far they can go.
3. Providing genuine opportunities for the child to succeed – this means being aware of the child's skills and interests and encouraging the child to achieve in those areas. The child may need a lot of encouragement to overcome poor self-image, and to succeed even in minor ways. However, successes are vitally important in raising self-esteem, and helping the child to feel good about herself.
4. Helping the child regain some control in her life, through involving her in decision-making, and listening to and respecting her views. It is tempting to want to over-'mother' a child who has suffered abuse, but it is more helpful to the child if she is encouraged to work some things out for herself so she can gain confidence in her own ability to make decisions and judge situations.
5. Deal sensitively with difficult behaviour (see the section on 'Dealing with Difficult Behaviour' above). It is important that the way in which difficult behaviour is handled does not further damage the child's self-esteem.
6. Be ready to listen to and share feelings with the child. It can be tempting to try and establish a fresh start and put the abuse behind you, but the child may need to talk about the abuse and the subsequent outcomes for quite some time after the investigation. This can feel uncomfortable and pointless, especially if the child seems to be going over the same ground repeatedly. However, it is an important part of the process by which the child starts to make sense of all the things which

have happened to him. The child may need to know your view, and it may in some cases be valuable to let the child know that you are angry, sad or upset that bad things have happened to him.

7. Show respect for the child's cultural background and interest in the events that make up the child's life.

Depending on the extent and type of abuse it may take a long time to help the child to start to feel good about herself. With some children it may feel like an impossible task. However, in offering this sort of support to the child at this stage, you will be contributing towards helping the child discover or regain happiness, confidence and the ability to enjoy life.

If the child's name has been placed on the Child Protection Register, she will have a key worker (usually a social worker) and be subject to review case conferences. In these cases it is important that strategies to help the child are discussed with the other workers involved. It may well be that you individually or your worksite (depending on your work setting) are subject to recommendations from the case conference in terms of monitoring the child's progress and supporting the child on a day-to-day basis. Talk over your strategies with others involved, especially the key worker, in order to share ideas and plans to promote increased confidence in the child, and to offer mutual support in dealing with particular problems or concerns.

Communicating with the Child Who Has Been Abused

Some children will be able to talk about their abuse openly and easily. However, many children have neither the skills nor language to express their feelings about what has happened to them. Some children may simply be pre-verbal, but for others it may be the enormity of the events which have taken place which are so overwhelming that they cannot be described. For other children, the denial of the abuse may continue after the investigation – some children can never talk about what has happened to them.

Children do not always communicate thoughts and feelings easily in words. We tend to be aware of a child's emotional state through his behaviour, demeanour and appearance, not because the child explains his state of mind to us. We often have to interpret how a child is feeling through non-verbal messages. For example, a young baby will express his state of being and needs (I'm hungry, I'm tired, I want a cuddle) through crying. If the child is not well known to us, it may be difficult to accurately determine what the message is. However, when we know a child well we are able to pick up the message more easily. This may be particularly significant when working with children with disability who have been abused, where the disability affects the child's ability to communicate. In this case, we need to be extra aware of the non–verbal messages the child is giving out.

A Chance to Think

 Communication involves the sending and receiving of messages between individuals or groups, and the interpretation of the meaning of those messages. We tend to think of talking when we think of communication, but in fact we communicate in a multitude of different ways, of which talking is only one.

Non-verbal communication is any method by which messages are passed between us that do not involve language. Non-verbal messages can be passed and received in many different ways. The term 'body language' is sometimes used to describe some of the methods by which we communicate non-verbally, e.g. smiles, hand gestures, grimaces, frowns, body posture (slumped, dejected, stiff, aggressive), appearance and image.

Exercise 5

1. Using the example of a young baby with no verbal language, list the ways in which you would communicate with her and examples of the messages that you would pass between you. For example, when we are cuddling a baby we will often smile at her. She will smile and make noises back to us, and perhaps wave her fists in the air or blow bubbles. The message sent, received and returned is one of mutual regard and affection, and pleasure in each other's company.
2. List the types of non-verbal messages you might get from a child in your care who is feeling sad and low.

Check your lists against the sample answers in Appendix II.

Children who have been abused need to express their feelings about what has happened to them in order to start the healing process. This can be an enormous hurdle for a child to get over even with help and encouragement. Part of our work with children who have been abused can be to offer the child opportunities to express feelings in a safe and secure environment. Many children will express feelings through difficult behaviour as discussed above. However, some children will appear not to express any feelings at all.

Non-verbal communication can be helpful in encouraging children who cannot, for whatever reason, speak about their abuse to express how they feel about it. You may be able to detect some of the child's feelings through the non-verbal messages he is sending out. For example, the child may appear miserable and uncertain of himself, be shy or withdrawn or obviously lacking in confidence, or be angry and aggressive in his manner and behaviour.

The child can be offered opportunities to express difficult feelings and emotions through day-to-day activities, in order to facilitate communication and start the healing process. Children who have very strong feelings may be quite frightened by the intensity of their emotions, and this may be a barrier to letting those feelings out. In order to help a child in this way it is important that the child has learned to see you as a trustworthy person.

The child may express feelings through play with dolls or small figures often in a typical domestic situation, e.g. the doll's house. The child may act out scenarios, e.g. one doll hitting another doll, sending a child doll to his bedroom. This acting out behaviour is common in young children and may help the child to start to make sense of what has happened to him.

The child may express feelings of anger through play. For example, one very angry 2-year-old little boy who had been separated from his mother after a long history of emotional abuse was causing problems in his childminder's home by behaving aggressively to the other children. The childminder tried to explain anger to the little boy by showing him drawings of an angry face and describing the feelings of anger to him in simple terms. She then showed him how to get rid of anger through thumping and kicking a big bean-bag. The child used the bean-bag to vent his anger and this seemed to help him behave more appropriately with other children.

Children can also express feelings through drawing and painting, and it is common among children who have been abused to indicate the abuse and their feelings about it in this way. It can be helpful for the child to make a picture of a particular event or to try and clarify a feeling. For example, one 6-year-old girl who was confused in her feelings about her foster carers and her birth mother who had abused her, drew a picture at her social worker's request of her ideal family. The picture contained her birth and foster families and she was able to explain that she wanted them all to live together as one happy family. Children will sometimes spontaneously reflect their feelings through drawings and paintings as the issues that are preoccupying the child will be at the forefront of her mind.

It may be appropriate to allow the child time to play alone as well as in the group and to sit quietly with the child while the play goes on. However, it is important to remember that there are no reliable interpretations of the meaning of particular images that the child might present us with and it is important not to over-interpret the child's message or look for meanings that are not there. Sometimes a simple acknowledgement is all that is required.

Finally, never try to force the child to communicate anything about his experience of abuse. The child can be gently encouraged but should not feel under pressure to explore painful areas of his life until he is ready. Some children will receive therapeutic help after the abuse and this can involve therapy through play or counselling, from a social worker or counsellor, which may bring out a great many feelings which you will perhaps see expressed during your time with the child. You may need to ask for guidance on what to expect or advice on concerns about the child's response from the appropriate person.

Conclusions

Each child that you work with will have differing needs, depending on the child's personality, life experiences and current situation. It is difficult to generalize about the needs of children who have been abused. Some will present as angry and hostile, through difficult behaviour and dislike and rejection of those around them. Some will present as sad, unhappy, withdrawn children with few communication skills. Some children will appear to be unaffected by the abuse, while others will develop superficial relationships with those around them and a chronic need to please. Much depends on the extent and type of abuse and the child's ability to cope, which usually rests on the level of support the child is getting. Child abuse will often change the child – his responses, his character and personality, his learning ability and his behaviour. Many of these changes will seem negative to adults around the child.

You may have to deal with difficult or confused behaviour or a withdrawn uncommunicative child. It is important to remember that often the child is expressing feelings which cannot be put into words, or acting out remembered scenes in order to make sense of them. You have a crucial role in supporting children in your care who have been abused, by helping them through their grief and pain and helping them move on. Perhaps the greatest contribution you can make to the child's progress is to demonstrate your care and concern consistently and persistently, because abused children need to know that they are valued and cared for over and above all other considerations.

Further Reading

Doyle, C. (1990) *Working with Abused Children*, London, Macmillan Education.

7

Protecting Children from Abuse

Introduction

The question for many childcare workers who are dealing with children who have been abused is, 'How could this have been prevented?' Perhaps a further question we might ask ourselves is, 'How can we stop this happening to other children in our care?' There are no easy answers to these questions. The level of child abuse in our society cannot be explained by the activities of a few 'bad' people. Children are abused because of complex interrelated factors (see Chapter 2), which are difficult to identify and change. In the earlier chapters of this book we discuss how individual workers can become more aware of abuse and more skilled at recognizing signs and symptoms of abuse. In this chapter we discuss preventative measures to try and reduce the incidence of child abuse. We will also look at how to help children to learn to protect themselves from abuse and to develop the self-confidence to know what to do if abuse takes place. Finally, we will explore how to create a childcare environment that is child-friendly and safe.

Most of the following applies mainly to older children who can comprehend some of the possible dangers of abuse and learn to respond to them. However, even quite young children can learn basic self-protection and simple responses to the threat of abuse. You cannot expect to prevent all possibility of abuse to the children in your care, but through these measures some children may avoid abuse, or abuse that takes place may be stopped at an early stage.

One of the problems that many children who have been abused may experience is the chance that they might be abused again. Abused children can become vulnerable to further abuse by the same or different adults, because they may have fewer defences and less trust in the protection of other adults. Children who have been abused need help to come to terms with what has happened to them, but they also need to learn the skills and attitudes they will need to increase the chances of avoiding further abuse. Children who have never been abused may also need to know how to seek protection or protect themselves against the possibility of harm from an adult or another child. Obviously children cannot always protect themselves, but a confident child who has a sense of self-worth may be safer than another child.

Teaching children how to protect themselves from abuse is an important way of helping them to recognize the difference between adult behaviour which is acceptable and that which is not. Young children learn the behaviour that adults teach them and they may well not be able to distinguish between 'good' and 'bad' adult behaviour until they are old enough to understand that not all families behave in the way that theirs does. Children not only need to be taught how to protect themselves but they also need active protection from any kind of abuse from the adults around them. This could include the policies and practices of a particular service, or could also include the way in which children are treated in our society more generally. Creating a non-abusive environment for children helps them to understand what is acceptable or not in the behaviour of others and themselves.

An increasing concern for professionals in the field of child abuse is the way in which abused children can become abusers themselves as they grow older. These children may not have received the help they need to unlearn behaviour that has been taught to them by the adults in their lives.

An example of this transition from abused child to abuser is Gary, a 13-year-old boy who lived with his mother, father and five brothers and sisters. Gary was sexually abused by various extended family members from the age of 5 onwards. By the time he was 11 he was actively involved in the sexual abuse of his younger brothers and sisters on the instructions of the adult males in his family. Gary refused to disclose his own abuse as he had been told that if the facts ever came to light he would be imprisoned for the abuse of his brothers and sisters. When Gary was moved from home he went to a children's unit where he immediately got into difficulties because of his sexualized behaviour towards both the other children and the staff.

Gary's situation seems to be increasingly common for children who have been sexually abused over a period of time. Part of our remit to explore the ways in which we can protect children is to look at how a child like Gary could have been helped to disclose his abuse at an earlier stage and to look at how children can be protected from abuse by other children.

One of the questions that is often asked by adults who become involved in child protection is why some children, who apparently have trusted adults to disclose to, keep the secret of their abuse. It can be very distressing for non-abusive carers to discover that their child was unable to disclose abuse to them, but for many children the threats that are made against them are real and terrifying, especially coming from an adult who has become so powerful in their lives that he or she can literally do anything to them. Children also often have a great sense of responsibility towards others around them and may feel that disclosure would damage the people that they care for. One example of this is a child who is being sexually abused by the father in the family, but who does not disclose to the mother because she does not want to upset her.

In this chapter we will look at ways of protecting children from abuse through the creation of non-abusive environments for all children and through helping children to learn to protect themselves. This will include exploring the needs of parents and the support that some parents might need in order to protect their children. In this chapter we will look at abuse in the broadest sense. There are four main areas to explore:

1. Preventing child abuse through good childcare practice.
2. Preventing child abuse at a societal level.
3. Helping all children to protect themselves.
4. Helping children who have already been abused to protect themselves.

Supporting Positive Childcare Practices

The Task of Parenting

Parenting is a complex and demanding job with some rewards and many responsibilities and duties. It is a tiring and often frustrating job with no fixed hours and little respite. It requires the parent to have multiple skills and an understanding of their own role in the healthy development of the child. For many parents the task is daunting to say the least. Parents of new babies often talk of the sense of overwhelming responsibility that comes with the arrival of the child and the corresponding fear that they will not be able to cope.

Like any other job, parenting has to be learned. For most parents the majority of this learning process is 'on the job' with 'trial and error' as a central part of the learning process. Advice is often given to new parents but may well be contradictory and confusing. There seems to be no blueprint for 'getting it right'. In addition there is an underlying assumption that mothers in particular will have some sort of instinct that automatically provides them with the skills and understanding they need to care for children successfully. It is no wonder that parenting is one of the most stressful jobs that we do.

New parents have to get to know their child, to learn about her personality and temperament, her preferences, likes and dislikes. They also have to learn to love her and to accept her as part of the family. For many parents this is not an instant process; it takes time and effort. Parents often experience disappointment that the feelings for the child are not immediate. This can seem like an anticlimax after the anticipation felt during the pregnancy and birth. Some parents may even feel negatively towards the baby, having feelings of dislike, rejection or even hatred. Bonding with the baby may not be an instant process but may take time. This can be very worrying for new parents especially if they have negative feelings towards the baby. Bonding may be hindered by early separations between parent and child, e.g. if the baby or mother is ill after the birth, or because the mother has depression after the birth, or if the father is excluded from caring in the early stages of the child's life.

It seems remarkable in the face of all these potential difficulties that anybody should be able to parent well. There often is no 'right' way to parent but many different successful methods of raising children that work for the families involved. However, there are certain requirements of the job of parenting that may not be fulfilled in some cases. Good parenting involves some knowledge of what a child can and cannot do at different stages of development. It also involves an understanding of the stresses and difficulties of the parenting role and a level of maturity that will cope with a physically and mentally exhausting job with often limited rewards. Abuse of children may often come about because the parents have unclear expectations of the role of the parent and what they can expect from the child. For example, the parent who becomes angry because the baby wets his nappy the minute he has been changed and assumes that the baby has done this on purpose to be annoying.

Some parents may have strong feelings that their baby does not like them because they interpret the baby's behaviour as deliberately aggressive and upsetting. Many parents have had feelings of failure when they have been unable to soothe their crying baby. In some parents these feelings of failure and a sense that the child is hostile to them may result in a poor relationship that could pave the way to abuse.

Example

A young single mother who had a painful birth following a difficult pregnancy fraught with concerns about the health of the mother and baby, took her baby home from hospital with no clear idea of feeding and other baby care routines. She had not understood the instructions given to her and had been ill for several days after the birth. Six weeks later she contacted the social services in an hysterical state announcing that she was going to kill herself to prevent herself from harming the baby. Her feelings towards the baby were extremely hostile. She said that the baby had ruined her life, deliberately caused her pain and that the baby hated her and would not be looked after by her. The mother demanded that the baby was removed from her care and said that she never wanted to see her again. During the work with the mother it became clear that her expectations of having a baby had been totally unrealistic. Alone in the world, she had felt that the baby would be someone to love, who would in turn love her. She had had virtually no previous contact with children and had no idea what to expect from being a parent. The mother attended a Family Centre with her baby where she learned basic parenting skills and gradually started to get to know and enjoy her child.

A Chance to Think

It is probably true to say that no one knows exactly what parenting means in practice until they become responsible for the care of a child. However, there are certain things that we can learn about parenting before we embark on the task of raising children. There is an argument put forward by some childcare experts that parenting should be taught to all children in school to prepare them for what will be a central part of most of their lives, in the same way that they learn skills and knowledge for the world of work.

Exercise 1

Imagine that you are planning a short course for 16-year-olds to teach them about the basic skills of parenting. Plan which topics you would include in the course. How do you think the course might contribute to child protection? Compare your plan with the sample in Appendix II.

Parents may not be fully equipped for the task of parenting and this may result in problems that could lead to abuse. Perhaps one of the greatest needs that new parents have is the uncritical support of other adults. For many new parents this support comes from each other, family and friends. It can mean respite from the demands of the child, time for adult company and own interests, time for the parents to be together and a sympathetic ear after an exhausting day. For many parents this support is a lifeline in terms of daily coping and retaining some sense of self.

However, some parents are more isolated socially and may not have the contacts they need to obtain this support easily. Young families living at a distance from the extended family may not get the support they need and single parents may be particularly vulnerable to isolation.

Example

Dawn was 18 when she had her first baby and the family row that attended the pregnancy and birth resulted in her leaving home when Anthony was 3 weeks old and going to live in poor quality, rented accommodation in another part of the city. Anthony's father initially seemed keen to be a parent but the reality of a demanding baby and broken nights horrified him and he disappeared from the scene. The relationship had been very brief before Dawn became pregnant and the father did not want to be tied down. Dawn became depressed and apathetic. She had no friends in the area she lived in and no money to travel to see her family. Often she did not get dressed or go out all day. Anthony also became apathetic, spending long periods of time in his cot, being prop-fed and remaining in soiled nappies for hours on end. At 6 months old Anthony had not started on solid foods and was showing no interest in sitting up or moving around. He looked pale and undernourished and he had appalling nappy rash. He was often found drinking fizzy soft drinks from his bottle. If he cried for long enough, Dawn screamed at him and shook him. She spent her time in front of the television in her dressing-gown.

Supporting Parents

There are a number of organizations which can offer help to parents who are not getting the support they need to cope well with the demands of parenting. Social services departments often have Family Centres where parents can get help to learn the skills to care for and enjoy their child. There are also a number of national and local telephone 'helplines' which offer support and advice to parents in difficulties, some of which offer further services to support the family. Health visitors will offer advice and support to parents on parenting skills and may also be able to put isolated parents in touch with local support groups. There are a number of charitable and voluntary organizations which offer different types of help to parents, some of them local and some national.

A Chance to Think

 For many parents it is very difficult to admit that they are having problems in parenting their children. To do so involves admitting that a task performed by the majority of us is too difficult. The parent may well feel that they do not want anyone to know of what they might see as their 'failure'. Some parents may be prevented from seeking the help that they need, because they feel ashamed that they cannot cope.

It is important to remember that parenting is a complex and demanding task and would be impossible for most of us without support and help. Parents who feel they are not coping may need sympathy and encouragement to talk about their problems and may also need help in seeking support. For many such parents the chance to talk with others in the same position about the way they feel can be tremendously helpful.

Exercise 2

1. Read the example about Dawn and Anthony again and make a note of the specific problems they both have.
2. Research services and resources for children and families in your area and note those which you think might help Dawn and Anthony.
3. How might Dawn get access to these services or resources?
4. What sort of support do you think she might need in order to ask for help?

Compare your notes to the section in Appendix II which describes the help that Dawn and Anthony actually got. Do you think the services they received were appropriate and adequate?

If childcare workers and other professionals are going to effectively support parents to parent well, then there must be careful consideration of how this might be best achieved. Research shows that the balance of resources allocated between support for families and protection of children may lean too far towards the latter. This may mean that resources are weighted towards investigation and following procedures rather than towards family support (Bullock *et al.*, 1995). One of the criticisms of the child protection system operated by social services departments is that investigations may take place and be followed by case conferences, but in the end the families involved may not be offered all the support they need.

In *Child Protection: Messages from Research* (DSRU, 1995) there is a useful analysis of the relationship between child protection work, family support work and child welfare. It is argued that early work with children and families should focus on their need for services. A small number of families will then enter the child protection procedures and this will result in either further child support or child welfare for children who have to be removed from home (see Figure 7.1).

Within the model in Figure 7.1 the focus would move away from investigation and towards support for families in difficulties. Investigations can leave the family less well equipped to cope than previously because the investigation is almost certainly going to add stress to the family circumstances. It may lead to conflict between parents and also with other family members. Parents may feel as if their lives have been turned inside out, their privacy destroyed and their credibility as carers completely undermined. To focus on the need for family support and services to help children in need may be a more fruitful approach, but will obviously have costs attached to it. Although child protection procedures must be followed where appropriate, it may be that by responding to early concerns about particular children with a 'family support' approach the likelihood of escalating concerns and the ever-increasing involvement of the child protection services may lessen.

So, what is your role in supporting families as part of an overall child protection plan? It may be that you might already have a specific role with certain children in your care within child protection procedures, e.g. monitoring the child's development or his physical and emotional condition. However, this does not prevent you from offering support to all parents as required.

There are a number of general points which may be useful when considering how parents can best be supported:

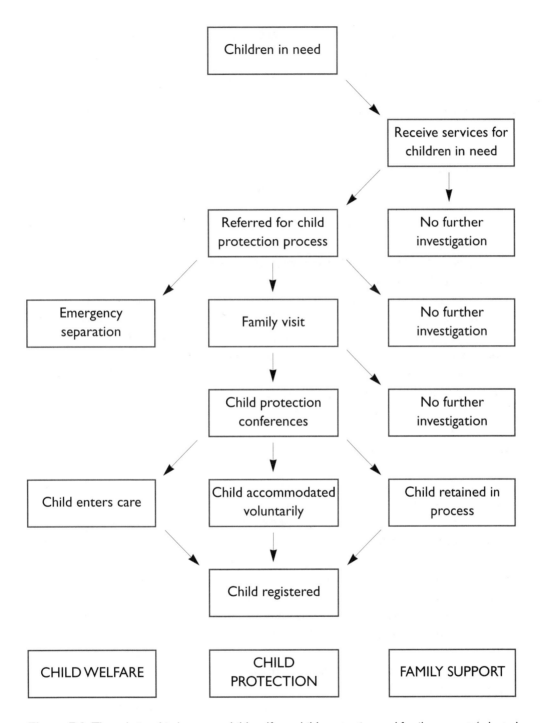

Figure 7.1 The relationship between child welfare, child protection and family support (adapted from DSRU, 1995)

- Focus on the needs of the child and family in a positive way rather than on any investigations which may take place.
- Blaming and criticizing parents for their lack of skills will not help them improve and may stop them using services that help them cope.
- Labelling parents as child abusers in our own minds or among our colleagues will not improve their skills.
- Parents may be hypersensitive to criticism after experiencing a child protection investigation.
- Contributing information to an investigation does not prevent you from also offering support to the family.
- Taking sides with the child or the child and one parent against the other is not going to help the child or family.
- The majority of children will remain at home after an investigation of possible abuse and you will have to work with the family after the event.
- Children may have deep attachments to parents who have poor parenting skills.
- The service you offer may be vital in supporting parents and diminishing the risk of abuse.

An example of how childcare workers approach parents illustrates the way in which negative messages can lead to problems.

Example

Diana and Tom were a young couple with one child, James, 3 years old. Due to concerns about James's welfare, initially raised by the health visitor, James had been attending a day nursery for six months to assist with his development and to monitor his progress. The nursery staff were in general not keen on Tom, who tended to shout at James and who was rude and offhand with them. They felt sorry for James, who appeared scruffy and neglected, and who often had a sad expression on his face. When bruises were found on James's back and legs a child protection investigation took place resulting in James's name going on the Child Protection Register although he continued to live with his parents. Part of James's care plan was to continue to attend nursery.

However, during his first week back at nursery after the case conference, Diana refused to take him on the third day because she felt that the nursery staff were judging her and talking about her. Tom took James to nursery instead, accused the staff of criticizing Diana, lost his temper and took James away from the nursery saying that he would never bring him back.

A Chance to Think

Parents who have become involved with the social services through childcare problems or a child protection investigation may well feel stigmatized; marked for the disapproval and criticism of others. This may make them feel extremely sensitive to the attitude and manner of others involved with their child. It can also be difficult for childcare workers to come to terms with their own personal feelings about their perceptions of the quality of parenting received by the children they care for. It can be difficult not to make comparisons between your own standards and those of the parents.

However, you have a responsibility to try and maintain a good working relationship with parents in order to be in a position to provide support and help to them. This may seem to put you in an impossible or even an undesirable position at times. In the end, however, the child is likely to continue living with her parents and working to support them can only benefit the child. In order to achieve this, personal feelings may have to be put aside during work time and dealt with either in supervision if you have it or with supportive colleagues and friends. Perhaps the most useful point to remember is that, as with children, we can reject the behaviour without rejecting the person. A parent who feels criticized or judged may well reject the help offered however badly it is needed rather than experience the judgemental attitudes of those involved.

 Exercise 3

Read the sections 'Dealing with Your Own Feelings about Child Abuse' and 'Professionalism in Child Protection' in Chapter 1 again. These may help you to think about the type of points you need to consider in terms of your own behaviour, manner and attitude towards parents of the children you care for. Then read the example about James and his parents again and answer the following questions.

1. List the type of behaviour the nursery staff need to avoid in order to be able to work with Diana and Tom.
2. How might the nursery staff deal with their feelings about Diana's and Tom's parenting of James more constructively?
3. What might be the outcome for James if his parents refuse to take him to nursery?
4. List the sort of help and support the nursery staff could offer James's parents and describe how this might also benefit James.

Compare your answers to the sample answers in Appendix II.

How can we actively support parents to develop good parenting skills? Your role in supporting parents will depend partly on your specific job and the type of involvement you have with the child and family. It may also depend on whether you have a specific role with the family outlined within the child protection plan, if there is one. However, there are a number of general strategies which it might be helpful to consider when planning how parents might be best supported when parenting difficulties arise. These are:

1. Developing a relationship with the parents in which they can share concerns and discuss problems in a supportive and positive way.
2. Sharing your own perceptions of the child's needs in a sensitive and thoughtful manner.
3. Listening to the parents and acknowledging the difficulties and problems they might be facing.
4. Emphasizing the positive aspects of the child's experience of parenting.
5. Sharing strategies for coping with the child's behaviour.
6. Presenting problems in a helpful, non-critical way.
7. Being able to offer information about other local services and resources which might benefit the child and his parents.
8. Demonstrating good childcare practice by example, e.g. helping parents to learn to praise desired behaviour in a child, or apply clear firm boundaries to behaviour.

Creating a Non-abusive Environment for Children

One of the ways in which children can benefit from your care is through the creation of a non-abusive environment in which they can grow and learn. This means one where they feel safe from abuse of any type, from adults and other children, where they feel respected and valued and where they can gain confidence and develop a healthy self-esteem. Clearly the form that this environment takes depends on the setting in which you work. If it is your own home you will have a great deal of control over it. If you work in an institutional setting, you will need to work within agreed guidelines or policies. However, there are a number of principles which can be applied to promote a non-abusive environment for children and to help them learn appropriate behaviour. These include:

1. Respecting children and teaching them to respect others, regardless of race, gender, culture or ability.
2. Presenting positive images of all children, through books, toys, games, posters, etc. There are still relatively few positive images of black and disabled children in child-care settings.
3. Develop clear guidelines on your response to bullying and attacks on children by other children. Often this behaviour is seen as 'normal' but it is clear that firm policies and responses to bullying do have an impact on the way children perceive their own behaviour.
4. Recognize and respond to racist attacks by children, whether verbal or physical. Strategies to deal with bullying should always address racism and have clear guidelines for responding to racist abuse.
5. Work in partnership with parents and share your approaches to maintaining a non-abusive environment.
6. Use praise to give children positive feedback about their efforts, achievements and behaviour.
7. Be aware of aggressive play and violent games. Children need to experiment through imaginative play with their images and perceptions of the world around them in order to make sense of it. However, it is important that such games are not a way of bullying or subjugating some of the children involved.
8. Treat verbal abuse and threats as seriously as physical assaults. Children can suffer dreadfully from verbal abuse in nursery or school settings.
9. Avoid negative comments about particular children. Labelling a child as a 'problem' will only reinforce his isolation and poor response to care.

A Chance to Think

 Children are sensitive to the environment in which they are placed and they will adopt the principles of that environment at an early age. A group of children will quickly recognize if a particular child is considered 'different' in some way and may respond negatively to that child. Carers can promote a positive attitude to all children through their own behaviour and through their expectations of the children in their care.

Exercise 4

Think about the care setting in which you work.

1. List the ways in which you are already promoting a non-abusive environment.
2. List the measures that could be taken to improve the non-abusive aspects of the environment.
3. What steps would you have to take to ensure these measures were introduced?

Childcare and Society

In Chapter 1 we discussed some of the social issues which influence the way in which children are treated in different societies, and how social structures affect the quality of life of children around the world. It is important to remember that many children do not have their basic needs met because of poverty, starvation, sexual exploitation, war and untreated illness, rather than because of the behaviour of particular individuals. Many children do not even have carers and may have to support themselves in whatever way is possible.

Societies can fail children by not providing their families with the framework within which they can parent effectively. Children often bear the brunt of social disasters and upheavals whether this is a drought leading to the starvation of millions, or rising unemployment which deprives families of the income they need. Children with disabilities are particularly disadvantaged by societies that fail to meet their needs or recognize their equal worth as human beings. Black children are also particularly disadvantaged by racist societies which label them as unequal in every respect and discriminate against them from birth onwards.

One of the ways in which the suffering of children is being addressed internationally is through the concept of 'children's rights'. On 20 November 1989 the United Nations adopted the Convention on the Rights of the Child. The convention is a list of the rights that children should have and which should be protected by governments around the world. These rights include the right to clean food and water, shelter and medicines, education and play, and the right to be safe and secure. For many children this is just a beginning in that the convention draws attention to the plight of children across the world.

Children's rights are also an issue at a national level. The concept of children's rights is central to a number of debates about how we care for children in our society. Perhaps one of the main debates regarding care of children in Britain today is the smacking issue. In Scandinavia there are laws which make the physical punishment of children illegal and there is a strong lobby in Britain today to have such laws in this country. The main organization to promote non-smacking is EPOCH (End Physical Punishment of Children), who campaign to have smacking banned. The majority of social services departments have a 'no smacking' policy for foster carers and childminders. Corporal punishment has long been banned in the majority of schools.

However, many parents use smacking as a punishment for their children. According to EPOCH statistics:

- Six out of ten parents hit their 1-year-old child.
- Nine out of ten parents hit their 14-year-olds.
- By the age of 7 one child in twelve was being hit by a parent at least once a day, one-third of children were hit once a week, and 22 per cent were beaten with a belt, stick or other weapon (*Daily Mirror*, December 1990; Donnellan, 1992, p. 20).

Other organizations such as the NSPCC support a 'no smacking' policy and argue that smacking can escalate into uncontrolled violence in some cases. EPOCH also argues that in 13 per cent of serious child physical abuse cases the cause lay in escalating physical punishment of the child. However, many parents still support mild physical punishment as a way of controlling their children's behaviour. EPOCH and their supporters argue that:

1. Smacking teaches children that problems can be solved through violence, thus breeding violent attitudes and behaviour in the child.
2. Smacking violates children's fundamental rights as people.

3. Smacking can lead directly to child abuse and is therefore dangerous to children.

Perhaps one of the strongest arguments against smacking is that adults can physically chastise children because the adult possesses superior size and strength. If we think of all the groups in society who are vulnerable to abuse we should note that inequalities in power and strength are a major distinction between abusers and the abused. Others argue that by making smacking illegal, parents will have their duties and responsibilities towards their children undermined and weakened. They argue that smacking is a useful way of showing children 'right' and 'wrong' behaviour and of stopping dangerous or destructive behaviour.

A Chance to Think

 Smacking has long been taken for granted as a punishment for children within their own families. However, it is unlikely that most of us would find it acceptable for other adults to smack our children. It is also probable if you are currently working in paid work with children that there is a 'no smacking' policy in your workplace or work setting. Despite this many parents' organizations, politicians and educationalists support the rights of parents to smack their children and argue that this right should be maintained in law. There are links here with the concept of children's rights because it could be argued that children suffer because unlike adults they possess no citizens' rights and therefore have no voice in society.

Exercise 5

1. Write down all the reasons that you can think of, or you have read about why smacking should be banned.

2. Write down all the reasons you can think of, or have read about why parents should have the right to smack their children.

   Discuss both sets of arguments with a friend or colleague and compare views.

3. What alternatives to smacking do parents have to control or alter their children's behaviour?

Compare your answers to the sample answers in Appendix II.

Helping Children to Protect Themselves

Children are obviously the responsibility of their carers and one of the responsibilities that carers have is to protect their children from abuse or harm. However, carers cannot be with their children 24 hours a day and it would not be desirable if they were. Children have to be left in the care of others and as they grow older they need to be allowed a certain amount of independence in order to grow into sensible, self-reliant young people. Carers often have the very difficult problem of balancing the child's growing need for independence and wider horizons and the need to know that the child is safe and secure. Media reports of child murders and abductions often result in children being kept in with their carers and chaperoned everywhere. There are no easy ways of finding the balance between safety and freedom.

However, one of the ways in which carers can protect their children is to provide them with basic self-protection skills in order to help them to be safer. Children can learn these skills from quite a young age and apply them to situations which arise in their lives. With growing concerns about the level of child abuse in our society, there has been an increased interest in teaching children these skills. There are now a large number of materials, including books, videos and games, which can be used by parents and teachers to show children how to protect themselves from adults who plan to harm them in some way.

The charity Kidscape has been central in raising the profile of child self-protection and creating the materials to assist concerned adults in doing this. The 'Kidscape Good Sense Defense Programme' founded in 1986 by Michelle Elliott and Wendy Tidman is a particularly good programme, partly because it focuses on the child's growing sense of self and the development of the child's instincts for danger, and partly because it does not focus on the idea that danger always comes from strangers (Donnellan, 1992, pp. 26–7, 30–1). If the materials used to raise children's awareness focus too much on the stereotypical 'stranger' – the man in the mackintosh at the school gate – then they may not prepare children for the possibility of danger from people they know. Much of this material is about the danger of sexual abuse and probably would be of little help to children in directly protecting themselves from severe physical abuse. However, the training could help a young child disclose abuse to another adult by helping the child to recognize that their carer's behaviour is considered wrong by other adults.

Programmes such as 'Kidscape Good Sense Defence' are usually used in schools with the carer's permission and involvement. They help children to know how to deal with basic problems such as getting lost; how to avoid being tricked into the power of strange adults; and how to fight and yell if an abduction or assault is taking place. These sorts of programmes place emphasis on building children's confidence so that they can trust their own judgement in potentially dangerous situations and so that they can learn that it is all right to break rules to protect themselves. Children are taught that they have rights not to be hurt or harmed in any way and that they should always tell another adult if abuse is taking place. Children are also taught to protect themselves against sexual abuse by learning the difference between touch that is acceptable to them and touch that feels 'wrong'. A great deal of emphasis is placed on secrets, because sexual abuse of children so often involves keeping secrets, something which even quite young children take very seriously. Children can be taught to know what is a 'good' secret (e.g. a birthday surprise) and what is a 'bad' secret (e.g. 'don't tell mummy we do this or she'll be very angry with you').

Helping children to learn to protect themselves can be a difficult task. Children need to know about potential dangers without becoming terrified or morbid about the possibility of assault. The age and level of development of a child is crucial in deciding the extent to which these issues can be discussed with her. However, there are a number of strategies for teaching even very young children self-protective skills as part of the daily learning process which child and family take for granted.

Personal Privacy

Babies obviously require intimate personal care from the adults they live with for a considerable length of time. However, as soon as a child is old enough there is no reason why she should not be encouraged to wash her own private parts in the bath with a sponge or flannel. Young children can also be encouraged to see their bodies as private and to decide for themselves who can touch them or not. It is important for carers to take note of the child's wishes and not to force the child to kiss or hug relatives and friends who he does not want to have contact with. The majority of the time the child will not want to hug or kiss Uncle Fred or Auntie Gladys because they do not like how they look or smell. Occasionally the child will have more serious reasons for wishing to avoid contact with a particular person.

Children should always have their own bed and should not have to sleep with an adult unless they wish to do so. Most children want to get into bed with their carers to cuddle up in the mornings, but they should always have a space of their own in which they can be private. Adults need to recognize and respect their child's growing need for privacy and modesty. Even quite small children ask for the toilet door to be closed, even if they later have to admit an adult to have their bottom wiped! Children are often instinctively averse to particular kinds of touch and handling, and their wishes should be respected in these matters. It is easy for adults to get into the habit of handling a child's body as if it were an extension of their own. Although children need physical care this should not mean that they have no rights over what is done with or to their bodies.

Example

Two girls of six and seven disclosed that they had been indecently assaulted by a 17-year-old male friend of the family when he babysat for them. The young man argued that he had only been treating the girls in the same way as their father did. The father admitted that as part of his play with the girls he did smack them on the buttocks and tweak their chests. There was no question of the father assaulting the girls – unlike the baby-sitter, there was no attempt to conceal his behaviour. However, the older girl did say that she had started to feel uncomfortable with her father's style of play and it was agreed that he should stop. The father admitted that he had failed to recognize the girls' growing maturity and that he still played with them as if they were 2 and 3 years old.

This does not mean to say that carers, particularly male carers, should start to worry about the implications of caring for their children's physical needs. It is perfectly natural and right that fathers should bath their children and put on cream and nappies, and wipe bottoms. Babies and infants will need these tasks doing for them, or help with these tasks, for several years. However, children should be encouraged to care for themselves at an early stage as part of their normal learning process and the move towards increased independence. At some stage a child will stop wanting to sleep with his carers and be bathed by adults, and these wishes should be respected.

Self-protection

Most young children are now routinely taught basic self-protection techniques by their carers. These usually include instructions

- not to go with strangers
- to tell an adult if strangers approach the child
- to yell, kick and scream for help if an assault or abduction takes place
- to avoid dangerous situations and to stay together in a group with other children
- not to be tricked into going with a stranger because she says that 'mummy sent her'.

Some families have emergency passwords for when another adult has to be sent to pick children up from school or social activities. Children can also be taught to check with school staff if a stranger arrives to take them home. Most children are also taught the boundaries of where they can and cannot go, and many are asked to check-in with carers at regular intervals when playing outside. All these are excellent strategies for helping children avoid 'stranger danger' but it may be that children need more indirect help to deal with problems closer to home.

Children will tend to trust the adults around them in a fairly unquestioning manner. They will also tend to believe that adults tell the truth and are generally to be obeyed as a matter of course. This is part of the reason why children are vulnerable to abuse from adults around them. Children are also afraid of being accused of being naughty and may well be easy to coerce into silence with threats of punishment. Children can also be very loyal and may keep the secret of their own abuse rather than implicate a family member. Children, therefore, will need help to sort out a response if the threat of abuse comes from closer to home.

Building a child's confidence and self-esteem will help the child to protect himself, as will building a trusting relationship with the child. Children who have a strong sense of self are less vulnerable to abuse, as are children who have good, supportive relationships with a number of adults. A child who is confident in the affection and care of the adults around her will have more chance of recognizing the motives of an abuser than a child who seeks love from any source. Creating a non-abusive environment for children (see above) may help the child recognize what is and is not abusive, and relate this to events in her own life. Good relationships with carers outside the family will give the child someone to disclose to if abuse is taking place.

Helping Children Who Have Been Abused

Children who have already been abused may be particularly vulnerable to further abuse from the same or different adults. The emotional and psychological outcomes of abuse can leave the child with few defences. Low self-esteem can contribute to this defencelessness as can the child's damaged perceptions of acceptable adult behaviour. Children who have been abused may crave affection and security and seek this within relationships with adults who are abusive. Children who are sexually abused may be particularly vulnerable because they may have developed sexualized behaviour at an early age which can attract the attention of abusive adults. The child's behaviour may be designed to please the adults around him in the only way he knows how.

Helping children who have been abused is a difficult task. Chapter 6 deals with the ways in which we can work with abused children in general. However, there are a few guidelines which you can follow to promote the protection of abused children in your care:

1. Be aware of the vulnerability of abused children and the possibility of further abuse taking place.
2. Ensure that the child knows all the self-protection strategies that she can comprehend at her stage of development.
3. Ensure that the child knows she can talk to you about difficult, painful and shocking issues without earning your disapproval or dislike.
4. With pre-verbal children be aware of possible signs and symptoms of further abuse (see Chapter 3).
5. Help the child build self-confidence and self-esteem through valuing the child and treating him with respect.
6. Gently discourage behaviours which may attract further abuse. Children who display sexualized behaviour need a great deal of support to change their behaviour and learn to relate to adults in different ways. Ignoring the behaviour may confuse the child. It is better to discourage the behaviour and offer alternatives so that the child has a clear message about what is acceptable and what is not. You need to be careful not to make the child feel that you find his behaviour shocking or disgusting in any way.

A Chance to Think

Helping children with behaviour that makes them vulnerable is a delicate process. Children who have been abused need to feel supported and loved. They need opportunities to learn how to feel good about themselves again. Discouraging certain behaviours can make the child feel unacceptable to those around him unless the process is dealt with sensitively.

Exercise 6

Read the case study below and answer the following questions.

1. How would you approach the problems of Peter's behaviour?
2. What other help might Peter need to cope with his feelings about the abuse?
3. What are the risks to Peter and those around him?

Compare your answers with the sample answers in Appendix II.

Peter is 5 years old. He has been placed in foster care after being made the subject of a Care Order. Peter has been physically and sexually abused by his mother and her boyfriend. It is unlikely that he will return to live with his family. Peter has some difficult behavioural problems which include sleeplessness, screaming fits, aggression towards other children and sexualized behaviour towards both men and women. This includes suggestive language and trying to touch adults' genitals. He masturbates frequently, often in public places including school. His carers and the school are concerned about the effect of Peter's behaviour on other children in the school.

Conclusions

Protecting children from abuse is not an easy task. It requires a combination of efforts on behalf of the child to try and ensure that abuse does not take place. Perhaps the most important factor is your own attitude and behaviour. Creating a non-abusive environment for children where they feel safe and respected is central to the growth of a child's self-esteem and self-confidence. This means having clear policies and procedures (in your own mind at least) about how you, or you and your colleagues, will deal with different types of abuse within the work setting. This will include racist abuse, bullying and victimization of children who are seen as different. You also need to recognize that not all abuse comes from individuals. Although an individual can have little impact on major social problems, you can be aware of the effects these may have on the children in your care. For example, as well as ensuring that your childcare environment is welcoming to and supportive of children from all cultural and racial backgrounds, you need to be aware of the effect on the child of experiencing racism and discrimination in the outside world. Discrimination may affect the child's image of self, his confidence and level of self-esteem. It may also adversely affect the child's behaviour.

Finally, if you work with children who have been abused you will need to be aware of their vulnerability to further abuse, and be prepared to support efforts to protect them.

References

Bullock, R., Little, M., Millham, S. and Mount, K. (1995) 'Studies in Child Protection', in DSRU, *Child Protection: Messages from Research*, London, HMSO.

Daily Mirror (1990) December.

Donnellan, C. ed. (1992) *Children's Rights: Issues for the Nineties Vol. 13*, Cambridge, Independence Educational.

DSRU (Dartington Social Research Unit) (Bullock, R., Little, M., Millham, S. and Mount, K.) (1995) *Child Protection: Messages from Research*, London, HMSO.

Further Reading

Doyle, C. (1990) *Working with Abused Children*, London, Macmillan Education.

Stone, M. (1990) *Child Protection Work: A Professional Guide*, Birmingham, BASW Venture Press.

8

Conclusion

You have finished the book. Hopefully, your knowledge and understanding of child abuse will have increased substantially, and you will have more information about your role and the roles of other professionals in the child protection process. Perhaps you were hoping for more concrete answers to your questions about child protection, but have discovered that one of the difficulties of working with abused children is that are no such easy answers. Looking back over the topics and exercises you have covered, you may be thinking that despite all your work you still have areas of uncertainty about your role in protecting children from abuse. Everyone who works with abused children has this sense of uncertainty at times, however experienced and qualified they might be. Living with these uncertainties is one of the skills of good child protection work, and one of the reasons why it is vital that you have support and advice from trusted colleagues or others when you are dealing with an abused child.

If you have read the whole book and completed the exercises you will have covered many of the important issues related to child protection. Many of the exercises are designed to promote debate and discussion about issues related to child abuse and child protection. Often there are no 'right' or 'wrong' answers. Protecting children from abuse is not an exact science – very often workers are having to act on suspicions and possibilities rather than on hard facts, and this may involve a delicate balancing act between differing needs. It is also true that in some cases, suspicions of child abuse turn out to be unfounded. Parents and children who are subject to child abuse investigations may well suffer from distress, anxiety and upset. In cases where no abuse is found, parents may be angry and outraged that suspicion has fallen on them. But, if the small possibility of 'getting it wrong' was to deter childcare workers from acting on their suspicions that a child in their care had been abused, many children would remain trapped in abusive situations, suffering increasing levels of harm as time passed. It may be helpful to remind you at this point that it is not your role to determine whether or not abuse has taken place. Your role is to use your understanding and awareness of child abuse to perceive the signs and symptoms and to report any concerns to the appropriate person. Remember also that many children who are abused by their families are protected in ways that do not involve permanent removal from their homes.

It is important to accept that there will always be areas of uncertainty in child protection work, and that these will contribute to the stresses individual workers experience when involved with child abuse. These stresses may be made worse by the fact that child abuse has a high profile in the media, and that professionals are sometimes publicly criticized for failing to act or for acting too 'heavy-handedly' when abuse is suspected. No one wants to end up with their picture in the tabloid press! Fear of 'getting it wrong' can cause childcare workers a great deal of anxiety. There are a number of ways in which this stress can be reduced to more manageable levels. First, knowledge and understanding of child abuse and the child protection process will help you to understand more of what is happening to the child and her family, and what your role is in this process. Being aware of the different types and possible indicators of child abuse can help you to have confidence to begin the process of reporting suspicions of abuse. Knowing the procedures and what will be expected of you might help to reduce anxiety. Developing skills in working with children and their families in difficult circumstances will also help you to make a valid contribution to the process.

Secondly, if you are involved in child protection it is vital that you are receiving support for yourself throughout the process. You may need to express angry feelings about what has happened to the child or what the parents have done. You may be distressed by the effect of the investigation on the child and her family, or worried that the child may remain in an abusive situation. Perhaps you have the day-to-day responsibility for the child and you have to support her through the process. You may be feeling that the other professionals involved are not responding appropriately to the suspected abuse, or that the investigation is taking too long or not reaching the right conclusions. Perhaps you are on the receiving end of angry or aggressive behaviour from the family because you initially drew attention to the signs and symptoms of abuse. Or it may be that you liked the parents and feel shocked and betrayed that they have behaved in this way. It is unlikely that you will go through the child protection process without feeling some level of anxiety or anger. Support can come from many different sources, but whatever the source you need to be able to discuss what has happened with someone who will understand the issues and who will be able to maintain strict confidentiality.

A Chance to Think

 For the individual childcare worker child abuse remains one of the most difficult and distressing aspects of the job of caring for children. Dealing with child abuse can evoke very strong feelings in childcare workers, which can be hard to cope with. These feelings need to be dealt with so they do not affect your judgement when dealing with abused children and their families.

Exercise 1

Now that you have finished reading the various chapters in this book, it may be helpful to turn back to Exercise 1 in Chapter 1 and look at the notes you made about how the subject of child abuse makes you feel. Have your feelings changed at all? What aspects of child abuse do you feel differently about? It may be a good idea to jot down a few notes about how learning more about child abuse may have changed your attitude towards working with abused children and their families. Hopefully, you may feel more prepared to respond to situations in which you suspect a child in your care has been abused. Perhaps knowing more about child abuse will help you to be less anxious about the possibility of such a situation arising.

Knowledge of the legal framework can provide you with vital information about the restrictions and requirements placed on the activities of other childcare professionals working with an abused child in your care. It may be difficult to understand, for example, why a child who you think has been abused remains or returns to the care of her family. Knowing that decisions in respect of the child have to be taken within legal boundaries may help to explain the outcomes for the child. In addition, you may have a role in the legal process, and knowledge and understanding of childcare legislation can help clarify that role and make it less daunting.

Perhaps most importantly, developing an awareness of child abuse in the broadest sense and using this awareness to develop a non-abusive environment for the children you care for is one of the main contributions you can make towards protecting children from abuse. Recent reports on the outcomes of the child protection process for children have criticized the lack of resources going into work designed to reduce the extent and seriousness of child abuse incidents. Preventative work with children who may be abused has had a low profile until recently, compared to investigation and procedure. Yet preventative work can go a long way towards identifying children vulnerable to abuse and providing the resources to reduce the chances of abuse taking place. Creating non-abusive environments for children could be your contribution towards preventing abuse taking place. In order to achieve this, consideration needs to be given to the link between prevention of child abuse and good practice issues.

Good practice relates to the values underpinning the care of children and the way these values are incorporated into the philosophy and culture of care in a particular setting. For example, this means thought being given to the way in which children from a range of backgrounds and cultures are treated as unique individuals, whose differences are respected and valued by those who care for them. Respecting individual differences, lifestyles and cultures means offering children an equal quality of service. In child protection terms this means conscientiously identifying and acknowledging our stereotypes and assumptions about which children in which families might be abused, in order to recognize and respond to the possibility of abuse for all children. It also means recognizing the disadvantages some children and their families may experience within the child protection process. For example, black children may have great difficulties disclosing abuse to white childcare workers, with whom they may have little in common culturally. Or assumptions about roles in black families may give rise to the tragic failure to provide appropriate services that took place with Tyra Henry's family.

Bandana Ahmed (1989) argues that for many black families suspected of child abuse there are two extremes in the approach of white-dominated social services departments. One of these is the punitive approach, whereby an inherent belief that black families provide substandard care to their children affects the way in which child protection investigations are handled. The other is the liberal approach, whereby high-risk situations for children in black families may not be identified for a number of reasons. These include stereotypical views of black families which may lead white workers to believe that some forms of child abuse are acceptable to certain black cultures or that these types of abuse are simply not present in those cultures. Worst of all, fear of contravening guidelines on anti-racist practice may persuade the workers not to intervene at all.

Central to the concept of good practice is the idea of individual rights and choices. Children often have limited chances to exercise rights and choices and, therefore, it may be the responsibility of the adults around them to uphold those rights. Perhaps one of the most fundamental rights is to live in safety and security without fear of abuse of any kind. Children who are abused often feel that they have lost all control of their lives and bodies, and it can take a long time to help such children to recover a sense of individuality and autonomy. Sadly, for some abused children discovery of their abuse can lead to the next stage of denial of choices and rights as the process of child protection rolls on without much thought to the child's wishes and desires. Although the Children Act, 1989, emphasizes the need to consult the child's wishes, this process needs to be seriously considered to avoid becoming a token effort. Effective communication with the child must be a top priority of all involved.

Good practice also informs your approach to parents and the quality of professionalism you bring to maintaining your relationship with parents during difficult stages of the investigation and response to suspected abuse. The need to maintain relationships with parents and to respond in a non-judgemental way towards them was discussed in detail in Chapter 4. It is important to remember that your response can open or close the doors to helping a particular family to provide better care for the child.

Good practice also relates to the availability of suitable toys and materials which provide images of various types of children, not just a few limited stereotypes. This is not always easy to achieve. There seems to be a very limited range of toys and materials which reflect positive images of disabled children, for example. The physical environment of the care setting needs to be suitable for the children who are or might be cared for in that setting.

Most importantly, the childcare worker needs to have the skills to meet the needs of different types of children and to recognize those needs in the first place. Developing these skills is dependent on a willingness to continue learning throughout your career.

If we look back over the twentieth century, it is clear that during this time much has been learned about the extent and nature of child abuse. In addition, there has been an enormous amount of progress in methods of identifying and investigating abuse of children, and developing child protection systems. However, child abuse remains a feature of modern societies, whatever definitions are used to describe such abuse. Perhaps the most important point to make here is that child protection systems are not static. As our knowledge and understanding of child abuse deepens and increases, the response to that abuse develops and changes. Child protection systems have undergone many changes since the early 1960s, and they will continue to develop into the future.

As such, childcare workers have an ongoing responsibility to maintain and update their knowledge and understanding of child protection issues. As a society, we are also becoming increasingly aware of the needs of our children and the ways in which we can care best for those children. However, despite improvements in standards of care, child abuse remains a feature of many children's lives. Part of the reason for this is that the nature of what is considered abusive to children is also changing over time. As standards of childcare change, so do concepts of abuse. This means that some of the childcare practices of today will probably be considered unacceptable or abusive in years to come. This may feel confusing to those who work with children and who therefore need a clear understanding of what is or is not abusive to them. As debates about particular aspects of childcare develop, it is important that those who have 'hands-on' care of children follow and participate in those debates.

One of the most interesting debates around children at the moment is the concept of developing children's rights, which was discussed in Chapter 7. There has been a growing movement across the world to identify and establish the concept of rights for children. Many of the arguments for children's rights link to the protection of children from abuse in the broadest sense, i.e. abuse by governments, institutions, poverty and war, as well as abuse by individual carers. Some would argue that the development of children's rights is the crucial next stage in reducing levels of child abuse and raising and maintaining standards of childcare. Since the late 1980s several local authorities have appointed Children's Rights Officers to give children living within the authority a voice in the services and facilities provided for them.

The children's rights movement may have particular significance for disabled children who are seen as less valuable and important than non-disabled children. This view is reflected in the lack of specific policies and guidelines for identifying and responding to possible indications of abuse in respect of disabled children, and for the persistent myth that disabled children are unlikely to be subjected to certain types of abuse. Some believe that the neglect of disabled children in terms of child protection reflects the low value placed on these children by society. Childcare workers may receive little additional help to develop effective skills in communicating about possible abuse with children who do not use an oral language. Sign languages can be too limited to express the details of an abusive incident, and a disabled child may not be able to communicate easily through play or drawing. Children with disabilities may find it difficult to access and respond to self-protection advice that may involve 'saying no' (not possible if the child does not use oral language), running away (in a wheelchair?) or kicking the offender on the shins! Investigating social workers who may be highly skilled in interviewing non-disabled children may simply not have the language to communicate with some disabled children. A review of training programmes and educational materials to include much more on how to respond to the abuse of disabled children is urgently needed.

Hopefully, you will want to continue developing your child protection skills through further reading, training or education. It may be that you are working or intend to work towards one of the childcare qualifications available, such as the NVQs in Early Years Care and Education or Caring For Children and Young People. This book is intended to provide appropriate background reading and preparation for successful assessment in such qualifications. Additional references are supplied for further reading.

Remember that developing your skills in child protection may be crucial for some of the children you care for. Building your own awareness of issues surrounding child abuse and child protection will increase your chances of effective intervention and your contribution to reducing the incidence and impact of abuse on the children in your care. Although your role in child protection is so important it is also limited. There are many other professionals to take responsibility for the protection of an individual child. Remember that you are not alone, and that it is necessary to identify your support systems, both personal and professional, for when you are dealing with abuse. Good luck!

Reference

Ahmed, B. (1989) 'Protecting Children from Abuse', *Social Work Today*, 8 June.

Further Reading

Franklin, B. (1995) *The Handbook of Children's Rights: Comparative Policy and Practice*, London, Routledge.

Northern Curriculum Development Project CCETSW Leeds (1992) *Anti-Racist Social Work Education No. 2 Improving Practice with Children and Families – A Training Manual*, London, Central Council for Training in Social Work.

Glossary

This glossary clarifies some of the terms and abbreviations used in this book.

ACPCs Area Child Protection Committees are composed of representatives from the main agencies involved in child protection in a particular area, with a remit to oversee the multidisciplinary child protection process, produce Child Protection Procedures and monitor service delivery.

Adoption Permanent alternative care for children involving transferring parental responsibilities to the adoptive parents whether contact with the birth family continues or not.

CAO A Child Assessment Order is made when assessment of a child is required but the parents will not consent to the assessment.

Care Order A court order under the Children Act, 1989, which gives care of a child to the local authority for the duration of the order (see Chapter 5).

Care system Refers to the various care arrangements for children of all ages, e.g. fostering, residential care, and the legal framework for these arrangements.

Case conference The formal meeting at which a particular child's circumstances are discussed and reviewed by professionals involved (and increasingly the parents) in respect of child protection processes.

Child protection plans The care plan produced for a child who has been abused which outlines how the child is to be protected, which agencies and services will be involved, and the procedures for monitoring and reviewing the effectiveness of the plan.

Child Protection Procedures Guidelines issued by local authorities outlining the roles and responsibilities of different agencies and professionals within the child protection process (see Chapter 4).

Child Protection Registers Lists of children who have been abused which can be accessed by social workers and others to check whether a child has been abused previously (see Chapter 4).

Child protection team All those professionals involved in providing child protection services to a particular child and family, e.g. social worker, teacher, health visitor, yourself.

CPAG Child Poverty Action Group is an organization which campaigns around a variety of issues connected to the deprivation of certain groups of children, and also publishes a range of books and reports on these issues.

DHSS Department of Health and Social Security (now DoH and DSS).

DoH Department of Health.

DSS Department of Social Services.

Dysfunctional Not functioning properly.

EPO Emergency Protection Order, formerly known as a Place of Safety Order is a court order enabling the applicant to move the child to a safe place.

EPOCH End Physical Punishment of Children is an organization that campaigns to have smacking of children banned.

Ethnic minorities A term sometimes used to describe groups of people from distinct cultural backgrounds who live among a larger, more dominant culture, e.g. groups of black and Asian people living in the white-dominated British society.

Foster care Care for children up to 18 years old in an approved foster family, lasting for short or long periods, where contact with the birth family may still exist although they are unable to care for the child at the time.

GP General Practitioner.

Guardian ad litem An independent social worker drawn from a local panel, whose role is to guard and promote the child's interests during court proceedings (such as Care Proceedings) and make reports to court based on a perception of the child's best interests.

Institution In this context this refers usually to a centre (residential or day care) where care is provided outside the child's home.

Inter-agency Between agencies, as in 'inter-agency co-operation', which means the way in which different agencies such as social services and education work together in a productive and effective manner.

Multidisciplinary In this context refers to professionals from a range of different services and agencies, e.g. teachers, social workers, nursery nurses, child psychologists.

NCH National Children's Homes are a national, voluntary organization providing childcare and protection services.

NHS National Health Service.

NSPCC The National Society for Prevention of Cruelty to Children is the largest organization for the protection of children apart from local authority social services departments, and the only voluntary organization with child protection powers within the law.

NVQ National Vocational Qualification.

Professionalism The type of behaviour and responses to others which would be appropriate in a work situation as opposed to in a personal situation.

Rehabilitated In this context refers to a child's successful return to his own home and family.

Residence Order A court order that states with whom a child is to live.

Signs and symptoms With reference to child abuse the term 'signs' refers to visible evidence of possible abuse, e.g. bruising, and 'symptoms' refers to behavioural indicators (see Chapter 3).

Social construct A term given meaning by the society that uses it at that point in time.

Social worker Usually refers to a trained professional who has a Diploma in Social Work (or Certificate of Qualification in Social Work) and is normally employed by a local authority

social services department, the NSPCC or another child protection agency.

Statutory Refers to organizations that are part of local or central government provision of public services, e.g. social services departments, education departments, NHS.

Stereotypes Assumptions and beliefs about a particular group of people, often based on external characteristics of that group, e.g. skin colour,which are then applied to all members of that group, whether relevant or not.

Supervision Order A court order under the Children Act, 1989, by which a child must be supervised by the local authority for the duration of the order.

Support network The range of formal and informal contacts an individual or family has access to which provides a framework of practical and emotional support for that individual and family.

Voluntary In this context refers to charitable or non-profit-making organizations which are set up for a particular purpose, e.g. NCH, NSPCC (see above).

Appendix I

Support for Adults Who Have Been Abused as Children

There is a depressing lack of comprehensive services to support adults who wish to find help with abuse that took place in childhood. Services tend to be patchy and fragmented, and to vary between areas. Below are some suggestions of services which may be available in your area. Your local social services department should be able to provide confidential information and advice about local services available or try the phone book.

- Incest Survivors and Rape Crisis are voluntary organizations providing advice and support to female survivors of sexual abuse.
- Increasingly, many health clinics and GPs' surgeries have a counselling service. The counsellor may offer you a service or suggest alternatives in strict confidentiality.

- The National Health Service (NHS) may offer psychotherapy or other types of counselling in your area although this varies. Referrals are usually through your GP.
- Many educational establishments now offer a counselling service for their students.
- Private therapists, counsellors and psychotherapists are available in most areas although you will have to pay for their services.

When choosing the help you need, it is important to be comfortable with the person who is offering that help, so take time to choose the service and helper who is right for you.

Sample Answers to Exercises

Chapter 1

Exercise 4

Question 2

The needs of children

Physical Food, drink, shelter and warmth, safety and security, supervision, protection from harm.

Emotional Love, affection, cuddles, praise, attention, positive feedback on achievements, support, respect, to be valued, to feel special.

Intellectual Play, learning alone and with others, being taught, stimulation of ideas and imagination, opportunities for new experiences, chances to explore, confidence-building.

Social Meeting other children and adults, a range of activities, learning to share, learning co-operation, learning acceptable social behaviour, making friends, developing social skills and confidence.

(a) Grant's physical needs may not be met when he is refused food as a punishment but, more importantly, his emotional needs may be unmet because he is shouted at too often and left alone for too long. This may make Grant feel rejected and unloved.

(b) Paul's emotional needs are not being met because he is not being given praise and regard, but he is being constantly blamed and criticized. In the long run this could lead to emotional damage.

(c) Claire may be suffering from neglect because of a lack of proper care and inappropriate feeding. Intellectually and emotionally she may suffer from lack of stimulation, and failure to bond with her parents. This situation is potentially abusive because of the lack of bonding and because Claire's mother is struggling to cope with inadequate support.

(d) Susan may not be getting her social and intellectual needs met because she is missing school and play, and she has too many responsibilities for her age. This may also affect Susan emotionally, because she is meeting the needs of others not herself. There are also safety and security issues because Susan is too young for the level of responsibility she has taken on.

(e) Natalie is not having her needs for safety and security met. She is physically and sexually at risk because of the poor levels of supervision she is getting. Although this situation may not be regarded as abusive, Natalie is in danger of coming to harm.

(f) Rena is suffering from abuse which may harm her emotional, intellectual and social development. The racism Rena is subject to could undermine her self-confidence and self-esteem and deny her social and educational opportunities. However, although Rena is being abused, this would not be the sort of abuse that would result in a child protection investigation.

Exercise 5

By representing images of the 'ideal family' we make an instant value-judgement about other types of family. Effectively, if two-parent nuclear families are 'ideal' this means that all other types of family are not. As a result there are many negative images and stereotypes of one-parent families, black families and families with non-conventional structures, e.g. where children are parented by adults who are not their birth parents. Assumptions about 'good' and 'bad' types of families can affect our judgement about which sort of families we are able to see as potentially abusive. We may be less likely to recognize abuse in an 'ideal' family than another type of family. We may assume that living in other types of families will automatically result in some sort of deprivation for children.

Chapter 2

Exercise 2

1. Physical condition – bruises, weight loss, signs of pain, general appearance.
2. Behaviour – changes in behaviour, any unexplained difficult behaviour, changes in eating patterns, clinginess, fear of adults, sadness, crying, withdrawn behaviour, unusual levels of anger or aggression.
3. Mother's response to Hannah – lack of affection, rough handling, hostility, indifference, negative comments.
4. Other factors – unknown people collecting Hannah from nursery, changes in family circumstances, e.g. mother has new relationship or gets pregnant again.

Exercise 3

Problems Gary's foster carers may have experienced in the early part of his placement might include aggressive behaviour, lack of concentration, soiling or wetting, repetitive behaviour, sleep problems, lack of confidence, regression, emotional distress, withdrawal.

Gary's longer-term problems might include enhanced learning problems, lack of confidence and poor self-image, relationship problems, anxiety, frustration leading to aggressive behaviour.

Exercise 4

It would be difficult to prove that a crime had taken place because the only witness is Norman. Because of his age and the problems of getting evidence on record that would stand up in court, those involved would have to determine whether there was any chance of a successful prosecution, taking into account the possible emotional effects of a court case on Norman. Although it is now possible for children to give evidence via video links, to avoid the distress of facing the alleged abuser in court, if Norman retracted his allegation and his sister and mother denied the abuse had taken place then a prosecution would be unlikely.

Medical evidence may show anal penetration had probably taken place, but this does not prove who was responsible. The main problem in proving child sexual abuse in court is that often the child is the only witness, and the process of gathering evidence can be extremely distressing for him. There have also been problems on some occasions in ensuring that the child's evidence is not disallowed, because it is deemed to have been distorted by adults during the interview process. Children can often feel pressurized to retract or deny allegations because of their loyalties to the adults involved, or because they have been threatened by the abuser, or because they fear separation from their families. The investigation process can be very stressful for the child, often resulting in confusion and anxiety. The child may have little idea about the outcomes of her disclosure, and may not initially realize that her allegations could result in police intervention, and possible prosecution for the abuser. Often children do not want the abuser to be punished, they just want the abuse to stop.

Exercise 5

Harry's grandmother may have felt that she had no choice but to provide a home for him, and this may have created resentments about having to care for him. She may need someone to discuss her feelings with, and to provide emotional support. A place at a family centre may have helped to ensure that Harry's care was better, and that he received regular monitoring. The centre could also have supported Harry's grandmother in her care of Harry, providing advice on practical childcare issues and a supportive environment. It would also be helpful to ensure that all benefits relevant to Harry were being received by his grandmother. When childcare arrangements are made informally, it sometimes happens that benefits such as Child Benefit are not transferred to the actual carer.

Chapter 3

Exercise 1

Question 1

Many people believe that abuse only occurs in families where there are obvious social and economic deprivations. Therefore, it is assumed that families who abuse are poor and that they live in poor quality housing on 'problem' estates, that the adults are unemployed and live on state benefits and are probably involved to some extent with minor or major criminal activities. Children who are poorly clothed or 'scruffy' may be seen as potential abuse victims. Children of economically stable middle-class families may, as a result of such stereotypes, be overlooked when they are being abused because they do not fit these stereotypes.

Question 2

Descriptions of the children in the pictures are as follows:

1. Leanna is the child of professional parents. She is well fed and cared for and has a huge number of toys, games and activities to enjoy. She has been sexually abused by her father over the last 12 months.
2. Peter lives with his mother and younger sister in a council flat. His father left a long time ago. The family has many financial problems and Peter's mother struggles to feed and clothe the family as well as pay the bills. The children have few possessions or treats, but they are loved and cherished by their mother and other relatives.
3. Susanna lives with both parents and her older sister in their own home. Susanna has learning disabilities and attends a special school. Since she was very young, Susanna has been beaten and kicked by her mother and locked in her room for long periods without food or drink.
4. Eddie lives with his mother and her boyfriend, who are both unemployed. The family live in poor accommodation and have had many moves in the last few years. Eddie's mum sometimes works as a prostitute to make ends meet, leaving Eddie for long periods with her boyfriend. Eddie has never been harmed in any way by either adult in his family.

Exercise 2

Have there been any changes in the family recently, for example, separation or divorce of the parents, changes in the family composition, a death, a new baby?

Is the child being bullied by other children or adults, or being singled out for ridicule or verbal abuse, for example, because of race, colour or cultural factors, or because the child is disabled?

Is the child struggling to learn or to make friends with other children?

Does the child have an illness or disability that may be causing distress?

Is the child being abused?

Exercise 3

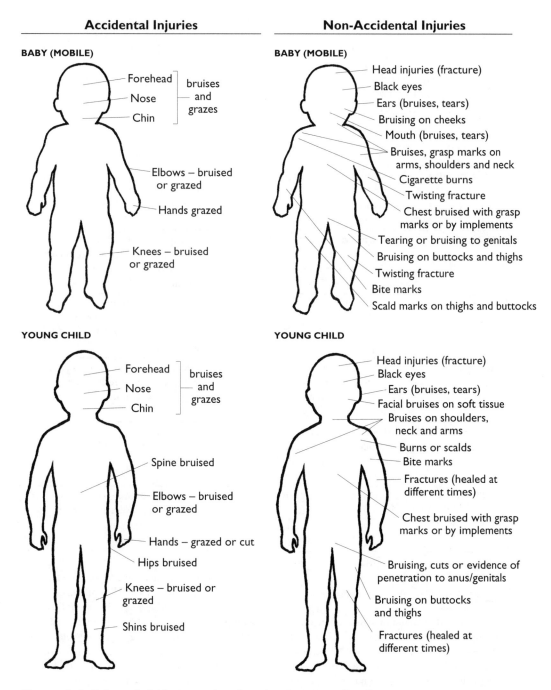

| **Accidental Injuries** | **Non-Accidental Injuries** |

BABY (MOBILE)

Forehead ⎱ bruises
Nose ⎰ and grazes
Chin

Elbows – bruised or grazed

Hands grazed

Knees – bruised or grazed

BABY (MOBILE)

Head injuries (fracture)
Black eyes
Ears (bruises, tears)
Bruising on cheeks
Mouth (bruises, tears)
Bruises, grasp marks on arms, shoulders and neck
Cigarette burns
Twisting fracture
Chest bruised with grasp marks or by implements
Tearing or bruising to genitals
Bruising on buttocks and thighs
Twisting fracture
Bite marks
Scald marks on thighs and buttocks

YOUNG CHILD

Forehead ⎱ bruises
Nose ⎰ and grazes
Chin

Spine bruised

Elbows – bruised or grazed

Hands – grazed or cut

Hips bruised

Knees – bruised or grazed

Shins bruised

YOUNG CHILD

Head injuries (fracture)
Black eyes
Ears (bruises, tears)
Facial bruises on soft tissue
Bruises on shoulders, neck and arms
Burns or scalds
Bite marks
Fractures (healed at different times)
Chest bruised with grasp marks or by implements
Bruising, cuts or evidence of penetration to anus/genitals
Bruising on buttocks and thighs
Fractures (healed at different times)

Figure A.1 Baby and child injuries (accidental and non-accidental)

Exercise 4

Question 1

It may be difficult to prove that a child has been emotionally abused because often the effects of emotional abuse are long term and, therefore, may not be immediately apparent. Those effects which are immediately apparent may be attributed to other causes, e.g. family changes, phases in growth and development, unhappy experiences. In the short terms, emotional abuse leaves no physical signs which can be used to establish that abuse has taken place. The parent's emotionally abusive behaviour may not be apparent to those outside the family. The child may be blamed for behaviour which upsets the family, even though that behaviour is a symptom of emotional abuse. Children who are physically or sexually abused usually suffer emotional damage as well.

Question 2

	Expected behaviour	Unusual behaviour
Leah 18 months	Walking, exploring, a few words, sleeping better, play, books, tantrums or refusal to obey instructions occasionally.	Lack of interest in new situations, fear of adults, poor use of play, often aggressive, withdrawn and unsocial.
Billy 3 years	Growing vocabulary, physically active, sharing play and new experiences, occasional outbursts, naughtiness.	Inactive and uninterested, socially withdrawn, poor speech, frequent outbursts, tearful, regressed to babyhood.
Jane 4 years	Learning numbers and letters, making new friends, active and energetic, large vocabulary, more independent.	Poor concentration, difficulties making friends, lack of confidence, fear of some adults, 'clingy', avoids learning.
Sam 6 years	Enjoying school, activities with friends, quite independent, doing tasks for self, physically active, controlling own behaviour.	Finding school hard, aggressive and/or withdrawn, poor relationships with others, lacks confidence, often disruptive.
Terry 8 years	As Sam above. Increased levels of independence, organized activities, socializing outside as well as with the family.	As Sam above. Missing school.
Eve 13 years	Activities with her peers, increasing levels of independence, some conflict with parents.	Truanting, promiscuity, drugs, alcohol, out of parental control, lacks confidence, aggressive or withdrawn, running away.

Exercise 5

Question 1

Young children of 2 or 3 may masturbate on occasion or appear to enjoy having their private parts touched during everyday care. Children often begin to show curiosity about sexual matters, e.g. asking where babies come from or asking about the differences between men's and women's genitals, when they are about 4 or 5. The child may want to look at or touch their mother's breasts or father's penis. Children of around 6 or 7 may play 'daddy and mummy' games during which they may look at each other's genitals. This curiosity may last for a short time or come and go. The child may lose interest in the subject once her curiosity is satisfied.

Question 2

A child who has been sexually abused may show levels of sexual knowledge and behaviour inappropriate to her years. This may include a complex knowledge of sexual acts, including oral sex, masturbation and penetrative vaginal or anal sex. The child may have a distinct vocabulary of words associated with sexual acts and may discuss these acts in a 'knowing' way. The child may make sexual approaches to adults, touching their genitals or making sexual suggestions. The child may be sexually aggressive when playing with other children, for example, grabbing at other children's genitals, trying to put fingers or objects into another child's vagina or anus. The child may masturbate frequently and publicly. Although young children may masturbate publicly, most 3- or 4-year-olds learn that this is a private act. Children who go through a phase of masturbating while young will usually stop when they get a little older.

Chapter 4

Exercise 1

Question 1

You might feel a sense of dismay that this has happened to you, or a feeling of 'not now!' if the timing is difficult. You may also feel worried about saying and doing the right things. You might feel that you would like to ignore the whole discussion or that it would be easy to interrupt the child and then the whole issue would be forgotten. You may feel a sense of relief that the child has started to disclose something which you have suspected for a while. You might worry about how you are going to face the parents. You might feel very angry or distressed at what has happened to the child and this may involve feelings of furious anger towards the person accused of the abuse. You may also feel exasperated that the child has put you in the position of having to cope with this disclosure. Your feelings are likely to be mixed and you may feel that you really do not want to be involved. You may feel concerned about what will happen next to the child.

Question 2

Your response might be to tell the child you are there to listen to her. You might then listen without interrupting, but using positive non-verbal communication to encourage the child to speak, e.g. eye contact, nods, an open expression and a relaxed body posture. You may need first to move the child to a more private place and to explain to the child why you are doing this. You may have to reassure the child that it is alright to give you this information, but that you cannot keep it to yourself if it involves abuse. You may need to offer the child comfort through words and/or touch if she is distressed.

Exercise 2

1. Interrupting can prevent the child from telling their whole story or give the impression of not being interested or not having time to listen.
2. Finishing sentences for other people can become a habit if we are permanently in a hurry, but we may not always get it right. Children need time to express themselves in their own way and at their own pace. There may be aspects of the child's story which are hard to tell and which only come to light if the child has plenty of time to plan what he is going to say.
3. Non-verbal skills are an essential component of listening. The use of eye contact, an attentive expression and posture and encouragement through small nods and smiles can be crucial in making the child feel that you are really listening to her, without interrupting the flow.
4. If we imagine we know what the child is going to say to us, we might miss the real message. We might even hear what we expect to hear, not what is being said to us. It is important to be sure that we listen carefully to the child's disclosure and that we report it to others in the way that it has been conveyed to us, without interpretations or assumptions.
5. Often we can miss crucial information from a child because we are too busy to listen. Children need time to express themselves and we need to make time to listen.

6. We can get into the habit of offering advice as soon as someone presents us with a problem. Although the intention might be helpful, this is not always the best thing to do. With children it may be better just to gather information and acknowledge that we have heard them.

7. Opportunities to listen to children come through shared activities, quiet play, bathtime, bedtime or story reading. The child needs your full attention and the sense that you are focused on her for the time being.

Exercise 3

Hannah will probably be feeling bewildered and afraid. She may be afraid of adult men and suspicious of strangers. Hannah might lack confidence and be nervous and easily upset. She may be sad and miserable. She might be afraid to do anything in case her actions provoke an attack.

Gary may feel rejected and unwanted, frightened, upset and angry. He may become very fearful of others.

Norman may be frightened of adults, untrusting and confused about what has happened to him. He may feel hurt, upset and insecure. He may not be able to place confidence in adults. He may feel betrayed and angry.

Harry will probably feel very sad and miserable, unloved and rejected. He may have feelings of self-hate and uselessness. He may feel unhappy and in pain.

Exercise 4

Question 2

You might start by telling the mother what your concerns are, simply and clearly, without trying to suggest what the problem is. For example, you might say 'I've noticed that Paul seems a bit upset lately and I was wondering if he was like this at home'. Or, 'Paul has been crying a lot lately and seems to need a lot of comfort'. Or, 'Paul has started wetting again and we wondered if you knew why this might be happening'. The idea is to encourage the mother to talk about Paul by involving her in your concerns.

Exercise 5

Question 1

- Avoiding getting involved.
- Thinking that it is none of your business.
- Not believing the parent is capable of abuse.
- Being friendly with the parents.
- Worrying about how the parents might respond.
- Not believing that abuse takes place in families you know.
- Not knowing what your role should be.
- Concerns that you will be responsible for the removal of a child from her family.
- Believing that social workers usually make mistakes when dealing with child abuse cases.
- Believing that the abuse will not affect the child much.
- Believing that the abuse is a one-off.
- Believing that you have to be absolutely sure that abuse has taken place before you report it.
- Not believing the child is telling the truth.

Question 2

- It is your responsibility to report concerns about the child.
- It is not your responsibility to decide if abuse has taken place.
- You believe the child.
- You may be saving a child from serious long-term harm.
- You may be saving a child's life.
- The abuse can be stopped.
- Most children in abuse cases are not permanently separated from their families.
- Help can be given to the family to make it a safe place for the child.
- If you do not report the abuse it will continue.

Exercise 6

Your report to the case conference might look like this:

> I saw bruising to John's buttocks and thighs on ... and I reported this to my manager because I was concerned as to how John had received the injuries. I also reported that John had lost weight in the last few

weeks and did not look very well. He seemed unhappy and sad. I also felt that John's mother might be having problems because she seemed angry with him and she did not seem to have much patience with him.

Exercise 7

Question 1

Discuss your conversation with a colleague or the appropriate person as soon as possible. Make a note of what Amy has said to you.

Question 2

As Amy is the subject of a Care Order, she will have a designated social worker. It is likely that you or the person you have discussed the conversation with will contact the social worker or her representative and tell them what has happened. The social worker would probably decide to talk to Amy somewhere private – perhaps your work setting. She would also want to talk to Mr Smith as soon as possible.

Question 3

This is not a potentially life-threatening situation so there would be no need for Amy to be removed from the foster home straightaway. However, if Amy was anxious not to return to her carers, or further information gave cause for concern, Amy might go to other carers for the night. Alternatively, Mr Smith might stay elsewhere until the investigation is completed. Other children in the family would also have to be considered.

Question 4

In the early stages, the social worker and her manager would be involved and also yourself and your manager if you have one. The social worker might decide to contact the police if she believed that a crime had been committed.

Chapter 5

Exercise 2

Question 2

1. Amy would be considered a 'child in need' because of her learning difficulties.

2. The only service Amy currently receives is her nursery placement.

3. Other services that might be considered in Amy's case are:

   - a child psychologist to help her parents deal with Amy's behaviour
   - a specialist nursery with staff trained to deal with Amy's behavioural problems
   - social work or volunteer support for Amy's parents
   - an educational psychologist to assess Amy's learning needs.

Amy and her family would be unlikely to gain access to all of these services, but these are the types of help that could be considered. All children with learning problems should have their educational needs assessed to ensure that additional support can be provided.

Exercise 3

Arrangements for Winston will depend on a number of factors including the extent of his injuries and the level of co-operation from his parents. The over-riding factor will be to ensure that Winston is safe for the duration of the investigation that will take place. Relatives have to be considered as potential carers, but if it was felt that they could not or would not protect Winston from further abuse then this option would be ruled out.

If Winston's injuries warranted a hospital stay then this would be the outcome whether an EPO was taken out or not. Winston could stay in hospital without an EPO if his parents agreed. If one of Winston's parents admitted the abuse and left the home temporarily, then it is possible that he could remain in the care of his other parent. However, the social worker would have to be sure that that other parent was not involved in the abuse and the he or she could protect Winston adequately. As both parents must have been aware of Winston's injuries then this is unlikely to be the outcome in this case. The most likely outcome would be that Winston stayed in hospital with his parents' agreement, and then was discharged to a responsible relative, who would not allow him to go back to his parents until such a time as Winston was seen to be safe in their care. Otherwise an EPO would be made.

Chapter 6

Exercise 2

Question 1

(a) Helpful reactions from the teacher could include:

- staying calm
- avoiding blaming Sheila or any of the other children
- telling a colleague as soon as possible
- keeping other children from knowing about the incident
- avoiding a panic reaction
- planning the response to the incident carefully.

(b) Unhelpful reactions from the teacher could include:

- showing negative feelings about the incident
- getting angry and upset with Sheila
- telling Sheila she is bad or naughty
- punishing Sheila
- punishing the other children involved
- showing panic or upset
- not seeking immediate advice from a colleague
- trying to keep the incident secret
- responding to the incident without careful consideration and discussion.

Question 2

Dos:

- remain consistent with Sheila
- include her in activities, games and play
- acknowledge her feelings of anger towards men
- be reliable
- be patient
- discuss feelings with the appropriate person
- respect her right to privacy
- check out whether physical contact is acceptable
- remember that she is a little girl.

Do nots:

- exclude Sheila because she makes you uncomfortable
- avoid touching her completely, e.g. putting her coat on
- touch her in ways she finds uncomfortable, e.g. bathtime may be best dealt with by others
- think that she can change overnight
- take it personally that she is afraid of men
- avoid acknowledging the damage the abuse has caused
- forget to set boundaries and limitations on Sheila's behaviour.

Question 3

You may find it difficult to cope with Sheila's hostility to your husband because this might put you in the position of having to mediate between the two of them. You would need to acknowledge that Sheila's dislike of men is based on her experiences. She has no reason to trust adults at present and it may take her a long time to learn to trust anyone again. You cannot expect her to feel safe with your husband even though you know she is. You will need to be sensitive to Sheila's need to feel safe, and to avoid insisting that she receives care from your husband when this is clearly causing anxiety. However, you also need to avoid taking on all the care, because Sheila needs to experience a good adult male role model wherever possible. However, Sheila will need to be given privacy and respect so that she can start to feel that her body belongs to herself. You will need to acknowledge the abuse has taken place and not avoid discussing it altogether.

Your husband may need support to cope with Sheila's hostility. You will need to plan with him how you are going to deal with the day-to-day problems of caring for Sheila, and how you are going to deal with her outbursts. He may need time to express his feelings about Sheila. You may need to help him understand that her lack of trust is not personal. You should both seek support from your social worker.

Question 4

If they are old enough, your children should be generally aware of what to do if either adults or other children behave towards them in ways they find uncomfortable or confusing. They should have a clear understanding of what is an acceptable secret and what is not (see Chapter 7). If the children are very young you may need to supervise play activities more than you would normally, although this should be as done as unobtrusively as possible. If you feel that Sheila's play with other children is inappropriate she needs to be told this kindly but firmly. She may need to express her feelings about the abuse in other ways, e.g. through drawings, through play by herself or with you. Make sure she has the opportunity. It would be better if Sheila had her own room. Try and teach her that she should have privacy but she needs to respect other children's privacy also. If you are struggling to deal with Sheila's behaviour around other children ask for support before the situation becomes critical.

Exercise 4

Question 3

(a) John is not having some of his physical needs met because he is sometimes deprived of food, and he is also sometimes physically chastised. John's needs to feel safe and secure are not being met because he is being punished regularly and he will feel insecure and anxious because of this. John's emotional and belongingness needs are not being met because he is not offered love, affection and respect. He is belittled and made to feel useless and unacceptable to his family, which will affect his sense of belongingness and will probably result in low self-esteem and a poor self-image. John's achievements are not being acknowledged and he receives no positive feedback or praise. This will affect his sense of purpose and his sense of being of value.

(b) John may be getting some of his needs met in school because he achieves in that environment. Teachers may praise him for his successes, recognize his achievements and encourage him to do well. John may have better self-esteem because of this and a sense of being valued. However, the positive effects of school may be offset by the poor value John's parents place on his successes in school.

(c) John will probably feel negative about himself, useless and unlovable. He may feel a sense of hopelessness and sadness about his future. He may blame himself for being unlovable, or believe that no one could love him because of some characteristic he possesses. John may see himself as ugly and unacceptable. He may feel that he is not a 'proper boy'. He may belittle the achievements he has made, because they are not confirmed by his parents. John may also feel angry and bitter that he is not loved and cared for. He might harbour great resentments against his parents.

(d) John's foster carers could help John's low self-esteem by praising his achievements and giving him opportunities to succeed. They should be consistent in showing warmth and affection towards him, valuing and respecting his views and opinions, and giving positive feedback wherever possible. They should listen to John and be aware of his feelings. If they have to discipline John they should make it clear that they are rejecting the behaviour and not John himself. They should be sensitive to John's worries about his masculinity and help him re-build his self-image by presenting him with a positive view of himself. John will need time and attention above all else. He may also need the chance to be 'little' again in order to catch up on the cuddles and love he missed out on as a younger child.

Exercise 5

Question 1

When we communicate with a young baby, we concentrate on the child's facial expressions and the sounds the child is making in order to receive messages from her. This could mean learning the tone of different types of cries in order to recognize a tired cry, a hungry cry or a bored cry. We would also notice the child's body language to give us a clue as to her state of mind, e.g. waving arms and legs could mean excitement or agitation. Smiles and giggles would tell us the baby was happy and having fun. In turn, we could communicate through words and noises, using tone to convey our message, e.g. singing softly to the baby. We would also make eye contact and use facial expressions to show warmth and love, or to amuse and stimulate, e.g. pulling silly faces. Touch is vitally important in conveying warmth, security and affection through cuddles, hugs, kisses and holding. Touch can also be used to entertain the baby, by tickling her, blowing raspberries, throwing her in the air and bouncing her around. As well as conveying warmth and stimulation, touch can be used firmly to denote boundaries or prevent accidents, or to prepare the child for practical tasks, e.g. dressing, nappy changing.

Question 2

Non-verbal messages from an unhappy child could include:

- drooping, defeated body posture
- little or no eye contact
- unsmiling, sad expression
- no smiles or laughs
- lack of response to external stimulus
- a hidden face
- tension or rigidity in the way the body is held.

Chapter 7

Exercise 1

Topics for a Basic Parenting Skills Course for 16-year-old Pupils

1. Stages of child development
2. Children's needs – physical, emotional, intellectual and social
3. Meeting children's needs
   - physical care skills
   - play and learning
   - social activities
   - love and affection
   - boundaries and controls
4. Personal qualities of parents, e.g. warmth, patience, maturity
5. Discipline
   - smacking?
   - time out
   - distractions
   - dealing with tantrums
   - being firm
6. Coping with stress
   - getting support
   - time off
   - time management
   - staying calm
   - sleep problems

Exercise 2

Dawn and Anthony received help from social services which initially involved a short-term stay in a foster home for Anthony. Dawn was prescribed anti-depressants by her GP. Dawn then received support from a volunteer with an organization called Homestart who support parents with childcare problems. The volunteer helped Dawn to attend a mother and toddler group with Anthony and to take him to playgroup once a week. Dawn made some friends locally and the volunteer helped her to make contact with her family again.

Other services which might have helped include:

- a nursery place for Anthony
- a Family Centre where Dawn could learn parenting skills with Anthony

Exercise 3

1. Avoid comments and attitudes that judge Tom and Diana. Avoid criticizing the parents. Do not ignore the problems the family has. Do not pretend the abuse has not happened. Avoid comparisons between your care of James and the parents' care. Do not exclude the parents.
2. Discuss feelings confidentially with colleagues. Try and recognize the problems the parents face. Recognize the positive aspects of Tom and Diana's relationship with James. Focus on how to help the parents to look after James.
3. James might lose out on the care he gets at nursery and the positive effects of that care on his growth and development. Tom and Diana may miss the support and help they could get from nursery staff and the respite from parenting. Stresses in the family may increase, raising the risks of further abuse.
4. Encourage the parents to share problems. Offer constructive suggestions for improving care and provide a good role model of caring. Share concerns about James with the parents. Give information about other services or sources of help.

Exercise 5

1. Arguments for banning smacking:

   - the severity of the smacks can escalate to the level of physical abuse
   - smacking may not be effective in changing behaviour
   - smacking is a denial of the child's rights
   - smacking teaches the child that hurting others is acceptable.

2. Arguments for the parents' right to smack their child:

   - parents should be free to choose their own methods of discipline
   - children need this type of discipline to learn 'right' from 'wrong'
   - smacking is effective.

3. Alternatives to smacking:

   - time out for parent and child
   - negotiation between parent and child
   - distracting the child
   - forfeits
   - praising wanted behaviour
   - ignoring unwanted behaviour
   - firmness.

Exercise 6

1. Dealing with the problem of Peter's behaviour:

   - accept that changes will take time
   - be loving, consistent and firm with boundaries
   - reject unacceptable behaviour, not the child himself
   - praise wanted behaviour
   - explain the differences between public and private behaviour
   - offer alternative models of behaviour.

2. Peter may benefit from work with a social worker, child psychologist or family therapist who is skilled and experienced in therapy with sexually abused children. This could help Peter to deal with some of his feelings and to learn to behave in more socially acceptable ways.

3. The risks for Peter are that he might be re-abused by an adult or older child who takes advantage of his vulnerable state. He may also become rejected or even ostracized by other children because of his behaviour and the stigma attached to children in care. Peter could be excluded from school and his learning might suffer. He may also experience problems later on in childhood and in adolescence.

The risks to other children include the possibility of sexual or physical attacks by Peter. Peter's behaviour may also be distressing or confusing to other children. Peter's sexual overtures to adults could put them at risk of accusations of abuse.

Notes for NVQ Candidates, Assessors or Training Providers

Linda Jones

Early Years Care and Education Level 3

The NVQ in Early Years Care and Education Level 3 is made up from the units listed below. You need to achieve all eleven mandatory units and three of the optional ones to obtain your NVQ.

Level 3 Mandatory Units

C2   Provide for children's physical needs
C3   Promote the physical development of children
C5   Promote children's social and emotional development
C7   Provide a framework for the management of behaviour
C10 Promote children's sensory and intellectual development
C11 Promote children's language and communication development
C15 Contribute to the protection of children from abuse
C16 Observe and assess the development and behaviour of children
E3   Plan and equip environments for children
M7   Plan, implement and evaluate learning activities and experiences
P2   Establish and maintain relationships with parents

Level 3 Optional Units

C14 Care for and promote the development of babies
C17 Promote the care and education of children with special needs
C18 Develop structured programmes for children with special needs
C24 Support the development of children's literacy skills

C25 Support the development of children's mathematical skills
M2   Manage admissions, finance and operating systems in care and education settings
M6   Work with other professionals
M8   Plan, implement and evaluate routines for children
M20 Inform and implement management committee policies and procedures
P4   Support parents in developing their parenting skills
P5   Involve parents in group activities
P7   Visit and support a family in their own home
P8   Establish and maintain a childcare and educational service
MCI/C1 Manage yourself (Management Charter Initiative)
MCI/C4 Create effective working relationships (Management Charter Initiative)

This NVQ is for people who work with children in their early years and with their families. In the UK, the term 'early years' is taken to mean children up to the age of 8 and 'family' means 'the group of people (relatives and friends) that are significant to a child' [Care Sector Consortium, November 1997].

Candidates working towards this award will find that many of the items of underpinning knowledge and understanding (UKU), required for competence across several units, will be remembered, explained or learned as they read each chapter. To help with assessment planning and evidence gathering a brief overview of which units are addressed in each chapter is listed below. The list is not exhaustive and the chapters do not set out to cover the whole list of UKU for any unit other than C15 'Contribute to the protection of children from abuse' which is addressed in the text as a whole.

The statement of underlying principles which underpin this award are integrated throughout the chapters.

Chapter 1

Mandatory Units

This section has provided some of the underpinning knowledge for several units which make up your award. As with all other chapters C15 'Contribute to the protection of children from abuse' is the central theme.

Aspects of C16 'Observe and assess the development and behaviour of children' is partly covered as the notion of normal developmental stages and appropriate developmental environments are identified.

C5 'Promote children's social and emotional development' is also covered in part. The impact of abuse or neglect upon normal developmental stages is touched upon.

Optional Units

M6 'Work with other professionals' – some attention is paid to the importance of the reader knowing the boundaries of their own role. This is explored in greater depth in later chapters.

MCI/C4 'Create effective working relationships'. The layout of the material and the time to think may improve your ability to reflect on your own development, further learning needs and seek feedback from others.

Chapter 2

This chapter has addressed aspects of the underpinning knowledge and understanding for the following units.

Mandatory Units

C15 'Contribute to the protection of children from abuse'. Detailed information on physical

behavioural and emotional indicators of abuse and neglect of children across the age range.

P2 'Establish and maintain relationships with parents'. Attention is given to the importance of parental involvement in cases of suspected abuse and neglect.

Underpinning knowledge and understanding, which enables the reader to identify how a child's development and behaviour may be effected by abuse or neglect, can be cross-referenced to several units including:

C2 'Provide for children's physical needs'

C3 'Promote the physical development of children'

C5 'Promote children's social and emotional development'

C7 'Provide a framework for the management of behaviour'

C11 'Promote children's language and communication development'.

Chapter 3

Mandatory Units

Again the UKU for C15 'Contribute to the protection of children from abuse' is addressed in some detail.

P2 'Establish and maintain relationships with parents'. The reasons for working in partnership with parents are identified in this chapter.

Optional Units

M6 'Work with other professionals'. Explanations of the importance of multidisciplinary approaches are provided in this chapter and the importance of each reader establishing the boundaries and limits of their role is identified.

Chapter 4

Mandatory Units

As with all chapters further learning relevant for the UKU of unit C15 is provided. This is integrated with aspects of the UKU for other units which require direct work with children and their parents in the highly charged context of child protection.

C11 'Promote children's language and communication development'. The importance of enabling the child to communicate and contribute to their future protection.

P2 'Establish and maintain relationships with parents'.

Optional Units

Aspects of UKU, which enables the candidate to identify ways of working with children and parents where there is suspicion of, or proven abuse, can be cross referenced to several optional units including:

M2 'Manage admissions' finance and operating systems in care and education settings'

P4 'Support parents in developing their parenting skills'

P5 'Involve parents in group activities'

P7 'Visit and support a family in their own home'

MCI/C4 'Create effective working relationships'.

Chapter 5

Mandatory Units

C15 'Contribute to the protection of children from abuse'. The legislative framework for child protection and the legal/policy requirements upon all participants.

C16 'Observe and assess the development and behaviour of children'. The UKU necessary for a candidate to contribute to a care plan for a child deemed to be in need. The importance of

observation and monitoring the effectiveness of interventions.

M7 'Plan, implement and evaluate learning activities and experiences'. The content of this chapter should help candidates reflect on how to ensure work with the child and family is both sensitive to the development of the child and meets the legislative requirements.

Optional Units

Aspects of the UKU and the legal rationale for at least two units are identified:

M6 'Work with other professionals'

MCI/C4 'Create effective working relationships'.

Chapter 6

Mandatory Units

C15 'Contribute to the protection of children from abuse'. How to identify and work effectively with the impact of the disclosure of abuse.

C16 'Observe and assess the development and behaviour of children'. UKU which helps the candidate recognize and monitor the impact of abuse and how to manage their own communication and work with the child.

C7 'Provide a framework for the management of behaviour'. Exploration of the reasons for and meaning of difficult behaviour and some methods and principles for managing it with the candidate own setting or for sharing with parents and other professionals.

Optional Units

Aspects of UKU, which enables the candidate to identify ways of working with children, parents and other professionals, can be cross referenced to several optional units including:

M6 'Work with other professionals'

P4 'Support parents in developing their parenting skills'

P5 'Involve parents in group activities'

P7 'Visit and support a family in their own home'

P8 'Establish and maintain a childcare and education service'

MCI/C4 'Create effective working relationships'.

Chapter 7

Mandatory Units

Many of the themes which emerge from the earlier chapter are revisited in this chapter – this time with an emphasis on preventative measures – providing UKU relevant to empowering the child to protect themselves. No new units of competence are addressed.

Caring for Children and Young People Level 3

Candidates need to achieve 12 units of competence to gain their NVQ Level 3. Candidates must complete a minimum of 4 units from Group A but may choose up to 7 if they are applicable to their work role. Where a candidate has not chosen 7 units from option A, then units from option B must be chosen to make up 7 optional units in total.

Mandatory Units

O2	Promote people's equality, diversity and rights
C15	Contribute to the protection of children from abuse
CU5	Receive, transmit, store and retrieve information
SC8	Contribute to the development, provision and review of care programmes
SC14	Establish, sustain and disengage working relationships with clients

Optional Units Group A

C7	Provide a framework for the management of behaviour
CU1	Promote, monitor and maintain health, safety and security in the workplace
M8	Plan, implement and evaluate routines for children
NC1	Enable individuals, their family and friends to adjust to and manage their loss
NC2	Enable individuals, their family and friends to explore and manage change
NC8	Enable one's own family and networks to support care services
SC9	Enable carers' families and networks to contribute to care services
W3	Support individuals with difficult or potentially difficult relationships
W8	Enable clients to maintain contacts in potentially isolating situations
Z8	Support clients when they are distressed.

Optional Units Group B

C5	Promote children's social and emotional development
C10	Promote children's sensory development and intellectual development
C16	Observe and assess the development and behaviour of children
C17	Promote the care and education of children with special needs
C18	Develop structured programmes for children with special needs
CL2	Promote communication with individuals when there are communication differences
CL5	Promote communication with those who do not use a recognized language format
CL6	Promote communication through physical contact
CL7	Promote communication and the development of relationships with individuals who lack development of social understanding and imagination
CU7	Develop one's own knowledge and practice
CU9	Contribute to the development and effectiveness of work teams
NC9	Represent individuals' and families' interests when they are not able to do so themselves
NC10	Contribute to developing and maintaining cultures and strategies in which people are respected and valued as individuals

NC11 Contribute to the planning, implementation and evaluation of therapeutic programmes to enable individuals to manage their behaviour

P2 Establish and maintain relationships with parents

P4 Support parents in developing their parenting skills

P7 Visit and support a family in their own home

X16 Prepare, implement and evaluate agreed therapeutic group activities

Y2 Enable individuals to find out about and use services and facilities

Y5 Assist individuals to move from a supportive to a more independent living environment

Z2 Contribute to the provision of advocacy for individuals

Z9 Enable clients to maintain their personal hygiene and appearance

Z17 Support clients who are substance users

MCI/B1 Support the efficient use of resources

MCI/C7 Contribute to the selection of personnel for activities

MCI/C9 Contribute to the development of teams and individuals

Candidates working towards this award will find that many of the items of underpinning knowledge and understanding (UKU) required for competence across several units will be remembered, explained or learned as they read each chapter. To help with assessment planning and evidence gathering a brief overview of which units are addressed in each chapter is listed below. The list is not exhaustive and the chapters do not set out to cover the whole list of UKU for any unit other than C15 'Contribute to the protection of children from abuse' which is addressed in the text as a whole.

The values which underpin all the units' O2 'promote people's equality, diversity and rights' are integrated and considered throughout the text. Also the layout and exercises are designed to enable the candidate to reflect upon their own learning, experiences, beliefs and values. Thus the book as a whole provides some UKU for the unit CU7 – 'Develop one's own knowledge and practice'.

Chapter 1

This chapter has provided some of the UKU for several units which make up your award.

Mandatory Units

As with all other chapters C15 'Contribute to the protection of children from abuse' is the central theme with some aspects of the O unit. Promote people's equality diversity and rights, considered in relation to protection from abuse.

SC8 'Contribute to the development, provision and review of care programmes' requires some of the basic knowledge about definitions of abusive and acceptable childcare practices identified in this introductory chapter.

Optional Units

Aspects of C16 'Observe and assess the development and behaviour of children' is partly covered as the notion of normal developmental stages and appropriate developmental environments are identified.

C5 'Promote children's social and emotional development' is also covered in part. The impact of abuse or neglect upon normal development stages is touched upon.

Aspects of UKU, which enables the candidate to identify acceptable and abusive ways of caring for children and young people, can be cross-referenced to several optional units including:

C5 'Promote children's social and emotional development'

C10 'Promote children's sensory development and intellectual development'.

Chapter 2

This chapter has addressed aspects of the UKU for the following units.

Mandatory Units

C15 'Contribute to the protection of children from abuse'. Detailed information on physical behavioural and emotional indicators of abuse and neglect of children across the age range.

SC8 'Contribute to the development, provision and review of care programmes'. This chapter identifies some of the basic knowledge about different types of abuse and the identification of how children can be protected.

Optional Units

P2 'Establish and maintain relationships with parents'. The reasons for working in partnership with parents are identified in this chapter

C16 'Observe and assess the development and behaviour of children'. Here the candidate's role in identifying suspicions of a range of abuse which might be affecting the child's development is identified.

Underpinning knowledge and understanding, which enables the reader to identify the different categories of abuse or neglect, can be cross-referenced to several units including:

NC2 'Enable individuals, their family and friends to explore and manage change'

W3 'Support individuals experiencing a change in their care requirements and provision'

Z8 'Support clients when they are distressed'

C5 'Promote children's social and emotional development'

C7 'Provide a framework for management of behaviour'

C10 'Promote children's language and communication development'.

Chapter 3

Mandatory Units

Again the UKU for C15 'Contribute to the protection of children from abuse' is addressed in some detail.

O2 'Promote people's equality, diversity and rights'. Some aspects of the UKU for this unit are

addressed within the chapter in relation to different cultural norms and attitudes to parenting and child-rearing.

SC14 'Establish, sustain and disengage working relationships with clients'. The importance of communicating and involving parents throughout any child protection investigation is explored in this section.

Optional Units

P2 'Establish and maintain relationships with parents'. The reasons for working in partnership with parents are identified in this chapter.

C16 'Observe and assess the development and behaviour of children'. Here the candidate is provided with information to support them in identification of physical, emotional, behavioural or developmental signs and symptoms of abuse.

CU9 'Contribute to the development and effectiveness of work teams'. Explanations of the importance of multidisciplinary approaches are provided in this chapter and the importance of each reader establishing the boundaries and limits of their role is identified.

Underpinning knowledge and understanding, which enables the reader to identify the signs and symptoms of abuse or neglect and the impact on other aspects of the relationship between the candidate child and his or her network, can be cross-referenced to several units including:

NC10 'Contribute to developing and maintaining cultures and strategies in which people are respected and valued as individuals'

NC11 'Contribute to the planning, implementation and evaluation of therapeutic programmes to enable individuals to manage their behaviour'

P4 'Support parents in developing their parenting skills'

P7 'Visit and support a family in their own home'

Y2 'Enable individuals to find out about and use services and facilities'.

Chapter 4

Mandatory Units

As with all units' further learning relevant for the UKU of unit C15 is provided. This is integrated with aspects of the UKU for other units which require direct work with children and their parents in the highly charged context of child protection.

CU5 'Receive, transmit, store and retrieve information'. Some attention is paid in this unit to the importance of accurate record-keeping to the process of child protection.

SC14 'Establish, sustain and disengage working relationships with clients'. The importance of communicating and involving service users, children and families throughout any child protection investigation is revisited in this section.

Optional Units

P2 'Establish and maintain relationships with parents'. Reasons for the early sensitive involvement of parents is provided in this chapter.

NC2 'Enable individuals, their family and friends to explore and manage change'. Helping service users come to terms with the involvement of a network of professionals etc. may be central to the role of many candidates for this award.

Aspects of UKU which enable the candidate to respond to suspicions of abuse or following a child protection referral can be cross-referenced to several optional units including:

> C7 'Provide a framework for managing behaviour'
>
> W5 'Support clients with difficult or potentially difficult relationships'
>
> Z8 'Support clients when they are distressed'
>
> CL2 'Promote communication with individuals where there are communication differences'
>
> P4 'Support parents in developing their parenting skills'
>
> P7 'Visit and support a family in their own home'.

Chapter 5

Provides information on the legislative framework around child protection and therefore is of relevance to many if not all of the units when evidence is drawn from cases where a child's welfare is a concern.

Mandatory Units

All, e.g. C15 'Contribute to the protection of children from abuse'. The legislative framework for child protection and the legal/policy requirements upon all participants.

Aspects of UKU, which identifies how the candidate's behaviour must fit within the legislative and policy framework.

Chapter 6

Mandatory Units

C15 'Contribute to the protection of children from abuse'. Explores the direct work with the child identifying key issues such as age appropriate communication and developing trust through openness, honesty and moving at the child's pace.

Aspects of the UKU for O2 'Promote people's equality, diversity and rights' are considered in relation to any direct work which the candidate might undertake with the child and or family e.g. the importance of recognizing cultural norms, confidentiality and managing conflicting rights.

SC8 'Contribute to the development and provision of review of care programmes'. The role of the candidate may be enhanced by reading this chapter.

Optional Units

This chapter provides information which provides the reader with the rationale and methods for direct work with the child and/or their family. It focuses on 'how to' providing practical knowledge, know-how and suggestions for practice. As such can be cross-referenced to items of UKU for any units which involve direct work with service users where abuse, neglect or failure to protect may have occurred.

Chapter 7

Many of the themes which emerge from the earlier chapters are revisited in this chapter – this time with an emphasis on preventative measures, providing UKU relevant to empowering the child to protect themselves. No new units of competence are addressed.

Index